The Mindful Board

Mastering the Art of
Conscious Governance

Charlotte M. Roberts and Martha W. Summerville

Published by Standing in the River Press LLC
63 Canner Street
New Haven, Connecticut 06511

Printed in the United States of America

Library of Congress Control Number: 2014912884

Developmental Editor: Nancy Breuer, Clear Magic

Book Designer: Melissa Blackburn

ISBN-13: 978-0692748930

HOW TO READ THIS BOOK

We have structured *The Mindful Board* to match different reading styles.

If you start at the beginning and read the headers, turning pages quickly, you will understand the overall structure of the book. You can go back to pages and chapters that caught your attention.

Or, read Chapter 2 to understand the continuum. Place your board on the continuum and go to the chapters that will help you most.

Or, if you're action oriented, read Part 2 first.

Part 1 answers the question, "**What is** Conscious Governance and the Mindful Board?"

Part 2 describes **how to** get started with each transition and stay the course.

We wish you an enjoyable journey toward the Mindful Board!

Table of Contents

About the Authors

Charlotte Roberts and Martha Summerville met almost 20 years ago at Guilford College, a small private liberal arts college in Greensboro, North Carolina founded by the Society of Friends (Quakers). They were both new board members and the next generation of trustees. "We began our commitment to conscious governance at this point, but we didn't know where it would take us." We have worked with boards and executives to enhance their leadership of the organization's mission. Our model of The Mindful Board has emerged and evolved through our work as board members, board chairs, and consultants.

Charlotte Roberts

Charlotte Roberts, Ph.D., has served on public service and educational boards for over 30 years as a way to "pay it forward." Throughout her career of consulting with and coaching executives, her work naturally led to working with their boards. She works across the critical boundary between board and officers to build their mastery of governance.

Her professional practice includes board evaluation and design, board training and development, facilitating board retreats, and designing special board/officers meetings. Governance is a weighty responsibility that can't be taken lightly. Board members must continuously build their governing capabilities to ensure the organization's future success.

Coaching executives includes building self-awareness through 360 assessment, executive presence, leadership development, and effective partnering with their board to achieve short and long term results. Executives who have to lead in multiple arenas benefit from her perspectives and experience.

Charlotte lives in the area of Charlotte, North Carolina.

Martha Summerville

Martha Summerville, Ph.D. has a passion for governing board development. Her commitment grows out of her service and leadership of governing boards for 30 years. As a board leader she has faced enterprise challenges as well as the joy of building a board from scratch.

As a board consultant, she focuses on strengthening capabilities to meet fiduciary responsibilities, align governance to business strategy, and respond to complex contexts. She specializes in board development, board leadership coaching, and customized board self-assessment. This includes conducting CEO performance reviews, facilitating board retreats, and coaching board leaders and officers.

In her work with executives and senior teams, she brings expertise in strategy development, organization design, and group dynamics as these leaders seek to adapt to industry and market changes. As an executive coach, she effectively supports executives whose roles are changing as their organization transforms.

Martha lives in New Haven, Connecticut.

You can contact Charlotte or Martha through the book website: themindfulboard. com.

Acknowledgements

This book emerged from a ten-year journey to build, test, and refine the path of Conscious Governance. We would not have made it to this point without a cadre of generous, smart, experienced people.

Martha Lamkin coached us through years of rewrites. Drs. Mel and Beth Keiser pushed us for clarity. Vic Cochran and Dan Mosca insisted on relevance to both for-profit and non-profit boards. Their patience fueled our perseverance. Seven people allowed us to interview them about their experience being an officer of an organization and a board chairperson for at least one board. In those interviews, we were able to test our model with Tom Chapman, Martha Lamkin, Hector McEachern, Anne Nobles, Ed Winslow, Jim Williams, and Art Zucker.

Nancy Breuer, recommended by Dick and Emily Axelrod after they read an early manuscript, was our developmental editor. Thank you. Nancy fearlessly advocated for the reader and ushered us to a different writing style and format. Nancy is not only a part of this book, she is a part of our consulting family. Art Kleiner, a friend and colleague, listened to us as our model evolved and offered to publish it in *strategy+business* in January 2016. His honing as Editor-in-chief, along with Dan Gross, got us over the mountain with the article "The Mindful Board."

Our clients have been true partners. We are grateful for their confidence in our ability to work with them as they tried new boardroom behaviors and forms. As their boards progressed, we could see more clearly the next stage in their trajectory. We pushed each other. They are the foundation under the fictional case study of Prescient that weaves together our book.

Finally, our families and friends have supported and encouraged us, even when they asked, "When are you going to be finished?" Our sisters, Frankie and Anne, and Martha's husband, Jeff, have served tea and sympathy too many times to count.

With humility and gratitude, we say thank you to all those who have believed in us and held us accountable for our commitment to exceptional governance in the boardroom.

Foreword

This book makes me want to serve on a board.

I admit that I already wanted to serve on a board, even before I read the book. Why not? You come into a room four times a year, with other eminent people, and you hear weighty questions raised about which you may or may not know anything, but you're treated like you're an expert with expert judgment. Then you offer your opinion, and the senior leaders of the enterprise pay attention to you. And maybe you even get paid for it. If it's the right kind of operation, you get paid quite a bit. If your advice is taken, and people follow it, you get to find out if you're as smart as you think you are. And if it doesn't work out…Well, there's always another board you can get hired on, now that you have experience.

It may have been cynical and fantastic, but that was my view. It assumed that serving on a board, like so many other things people do in business, was more or less unconscious.

Charlotte Roberts and Martha Summerville show, in this book, that governance is extraordinarily conscious—at least when it's done right. In fact, a really good board of directors or advisory board is a vehicle for becoming more conscious: as individual members, and as an organization. Now that I see the difference, this book makes me want to serve on a board in the right way, for the right reason, with the right people. For in the real world—as opposed to in my fantasy—a board is a construction designed to provide leaders of with the perspective they need to monitor and improve their organizations, and thus to make the world a better place.

You may ask why organizations are so important to civilization. I think many people underestimate the extent to which they influence the events that shape humanity. Very few human endeavors are managed alone. Even something as solitary as writing a book is not truly a solitary act. It may not take a village to write a book, but it takes an organization to publish one. Or, if it's self-published, it takes an organization to distribute one. And the readers of the book, if they are moved to act, become a sort of impromptu organization. And if they are truly moved to change the world in any significant way, then they will have to specialize, because no one can do it all alone, not any act that's complicated. They will have to choose a few of them to coordinate how they all operate together, and then the people who are coordinating, who are conducting this impromptu orchestra, will have to figure out a way to support themselves or get recognized, which means they'll have to have functional expertise and reporting structures, and then the question will come up that inevitably comes up: How do we manage the fact that all human beings, even leaders, are fallible? And so, before you know it, there will be the need for a board.

Great organizations need great boards. Some great organizations, it is said, don't have great boards. They have great CEOs, whose boards simply rubber-stamp what the CEOs tell them to do. But those are not sustainably great organizations. They are lucky. When their luck runs out, they will need a board to pick up the pieces.

This is a book about how to pick up the pieces, if you're on a board. Or how to imagine picking up the pieces, if, like me, you're merely a board wannabe. Or, even better, to take responsibility for your board's evolution before a crash and not have to pick up any pieces at all.

I don't want to kill the suspense of the book, so I'm not going to give away too much of the methodology that the authors are about to bring you. But I can say this much: It starts with taking true notice of the value of one's own counsel and guidance. It means being proud with the right amount of humility, helpful with the proper dose of abrasive objectivity, and able to think through ramifications while being narrowly focused on the value of this group. It means having all the status and none of the status, being in charge and not in charge. In short, it means recognizing the power of truly generative conversations, and being able to bring those conversations to bear when needed.

It's an art, and like all truly great arts, there's a lot of science and methodology backing it up. In this case, the science is the science of human nature. Boards are groups, and groups are, in a very real sense, sentient creatures. That is, if they exist for any length of time, they take on a mind of their own, independent of the thoughts of any individual who happens to sit on the board. The board is not a rubber-stamp for the CEO; the board is a room where the CEO—and other leaders of the enterprise—go to show that they are truly worthy of the trust placed in them.

Can you be a member of that sort of board? Not without practice. You'll need a bit of perspective, but practice is the important thing. You're a board member even on the days when you don't show up for meetings. You are constantly committed to the enterprise. Your relationship with it is the instrument you bring to the orchestra—or, if it's a different type of organization, to the jazz band.

Charlotte Roberts and Martha Summerville are people who understand boards, in part, because they have made that kind of commitment. They understand the traditions that have led to board quality, in part because of their familiarity with Quaker ideas, where board membership is like combining collective responsibility with conscious enlightenment. Although their experience is hardly limited to one group's thinking: it is broad, and universal. They explain in this book where Conscious Governance comes from—and then they take you as close to experiencing it as any book can. With this book, you can be far more effective on the boards you sit on now, and ready for the call, whenever it may come.

Art Kleiner

PwC | Editor-in-chief, *strategy+business*

PART 1: KNOW THE MODEL

Welcome!

You have chosen to explore this book. Doing so places you on the path to the Mindful Board. You are about to start a journey. To prepare for the journey you will need these virtual supplies:

- A notebook and pen—to capture your thoughts

- A mirror—to look inside yourself along the way

- A panoramic lens—to expand your perspective

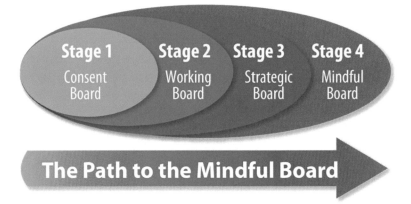

Part 1 introduces you to Conscious Governance and the path to the Mindful Board.

- **Chapter 1** describes why *Conscious Governance* is the new demand of the 21st century.

- **Chapter 2** defines the *four stages on the path* to the Mindful Board.

- **Chapter 3** is a deep dive into the *six vital disciplines* of Conscious Governance.

- **Chapter 4** shows you the *six powerful tools* you will use to transform your board.

- **Chapter 5** invites you to become a *mindful board member.*

Step onto the path that crosses the landscape of Conscious Governance.

Chapter 1

Break the Constraints:
Your Governance Model Is Holding You Back

The old corporation was one of the singular successes of the 20th century, creating vast amounts of wealth and prosperity around the globe. The new corporation will be something different. But what? Optimists see a more responsive, more democratic, more socially responsible institution emerging from the upheaval. Pessimists fear that the very same ills that plague modern-day politics—polarization, divisiveness, and stalemate—may come to hobble corporation. ... The dramatic power struggles that now are playing out in the CEO suite and the boardroom will, in the end, determine what kinds of lives and what kind of world our children and our children's children inherit.

— Alan Murray, *Revolt in the Boardroom*

The Scorched Platform:
The Need to Transform Governance is Old News

Governance is a Promise

Governance is a promise to serve the best interest of the enterprise and those impacted by its products, services, and activities that will affect them for as long as the enterprise exists—even beyond the life of the organization. Today the impact of governance stretches out further, far beyond the traditional boundaries of sectors, markets, regions and nations.

As economies interact and the external context changes, boards must choose a governance model that makes it possible for them, individually and collectively, to fulfill their promise to stakeholders, shareholders and beyond. Because the quality and effectiveness of governance is directly tied to the quality of leadership inside the organization, choosing the right model for the enterprise is essential.

Any group of people involved in making decisions for a system is involved in governance—the group makes a promise to the system they serve. Whether we are talking about a school board, PTA, church elders, city council, global corporation or an investment committee, these groups make an implicit or explicit promise to their stakeholders and the public good. In this book we focus on governing boards (for-profit and non-profit) because their actions put them in the public eye.

Read with Both You and Your Board in Mind

Do you serve on a board? Do you want to see your board change the way it stewards the mission and vision of the enterprise?

Governance has substance, carries responsibility, demands leadership, and evokes a desire to serve—maybe even to leave a legacy. Serving is a privilege and responsibility, not just a stepping stone or a boost to rank, social status, or income. While an individual may benefit, board service is bigger than any one of us and the impact of board deliberations is often greater than we anticipate. Your presence in the boardroom matters; you and a group of committed colleagues have the power to transform governance from any chair whether you are on the executive committee or a member at large.

You and a group of committed colleagues have the power to transform governance from any chair whether you are on the executive committee or a member at large.

As you read, you will compare the board you are serving on to the four types of boards in our model of Conscious Governance. Think about which type of board best fits the needs of your organization. Also consider which type of board best fits your work style.

Throughout this book you will discover ways to be a productive member and contribute in meetings. You will also learn how to help the board become the Mindful Board through building capabilities and transforming its purpose and tasks. Take your time integrating these ideas.

Welcome to the Era of Conscious Governance

For several decades, experts and practitioners have debated the quality of governing boards and the effectiveness of their governance. Set against a backdrop of disappointment, sometimes anger, at governance failures and poor board performance, many people realize that boards need to change dramatically. Boards need to be exceptional, relevant, productive, purposeful and "leaderful."[1]

Conscious Governance Aligns with Complex Realities

Current available models are not sufficient to resolve the complex challenges. Learning to practice Conscious Governance will put you on the path to a form of governance better matched to the demands of the 21st century.

Conscious Governance is a three-part commitment:

1. To govern in the best interest of the organization and those impacted by its activities.

2. To invest in the ongoing development of the board's capabilities.

3. To acknowledge continuous change in complex systems and respond appropriately to signals of changing contexts (internal and external).

Conscious Governance drives necessary transformation in the work and identity of the board (or other key decision-making groups) to serve the organization in its new context and circumstances.

The heart of Conscious Governance is the imperative to lead as an integrated, high functioning *cohesive group with collective consciousness and shared purpose.* The quality of governance impacts the organization's performance. A board unable to recognize the need for change or unwilling to transform their governance practices to fit new contexts thwarts the organization's likelihood of thriving long term.

Governance Has Been Forced to Change

Patronage, stewardship and the protecting role of governance are long-standing traditions rich with explicit and implicit values and responsibilities. In his book *Entrusted: The Moral Responsibilities of Trusteeship* David Smith reminds us "Trusteeship as a form of relationship arose in Roman law and has been refined in England and America [over many years]." Many traditions and assumptions asso-

---

[1] See Joseph Raelin's work on "leaderful" organizations in *Creating the Leaderful Organization*

ciated with the history of governance are under scrutiny. The governance scandals that came to light around the turn of the 21st century pushed the private world of governance into the nightly news. Tyco, WorldCom, and Enron are perhaps the most infamous for-profit cases, but they were certainly not the only serious governance failures. Governance debacles have touched higher education (such as American University and Penn State University), healthcare, and many non-profit service organizations including The Red Cross. Certainly the banking debacle of 2008 had deeper economic impact and raised serious governance questions. The scandals and outrage associated with them continue across every industry and sector.

One result of the front-page news has been a burst of interest in how boards can change and develop, generating a wave of books, articles, workshops, and "how-to" manuals. All of these reflect a very serious effort to create and implement models and strategies to achieve effective governance.

The recent Great Recession (2008-2013) brought with it another round of governance oversight gaps and missteps. Questions emerged: To whom or what do boards owe loyalty? How can self-serving or poorly performing boards be prompted to reform? How should boards relate to regulators and large investors—each with power over the organization?

At the same time, new types of corporations and forms of business are emerging and flourishing across the globe. Consider the benefit-corporation movement, the growth of social entrepreneurship, the continued revolution and reinvention of online business, and the increasingly varied forms of partnerships across industries. The business revolution brings with it a demand for 21st century governance.

B-Corps are for-profit companies that intentionally serve both shareholders and society. They produce financial returns while creating a material positive impact on society and the environment. Some people see this form of doing business as the evolution of capitalism, using business for the good of the world.

B Lab is a non-profit organization that wants to redefine success in business. They may be engaged to assess and certify that a company meets their rigorous standards of social and environmental performance, accountability, and transparency. But certification is not required to be a Benefit Corporation. Many states now have B-Corp provisions. The fiduciary duties of a B-Corp board are expanded to include public benefit.

The question now is:

• Are the available models and approaches to board development enough to resolve the challenges and opportunities of the 21st century?

Incremental Change Won't Work Anymore

Contexts are changing. Power struggles are erupting. The board-officer boundary is being challenged. Board chairs have said they want more officer responsiveness to their requests as well as officers' acceptance of the board securing outside opinions. We hear CEOs lament how their boards need to be more engaged and better prepared to think strategically. We hear officers express despair at their loss of control of the board. We have heard boards complain of loss of control of the CEO and officers. Sometimes we hear both sides of the governance line in an organization complaining about the other side. In all these situations, the organization suffers. The evolving relationship between board and officers is vital and demands a crucial conversation.

Simple solutions are to expand the board's agenda, evaluate the board's capability, and add new members with specific skills and expertise. In a 2014 newsletter, for example, Casal and Caspar of McKinsey & Company argue the case of the "forward-looking board," one that spends more time, energy and investment in the zone of strategy. The advice implies that directors need to work harder. Ram Charan, Denis Carey and Michael Useem expand the boundary of board duties to include the "duty of leadership" in their 2014 book, *Boards That Lead: When to Take Charge, When to Partner, and When to Stay Out of the Way.* Conscientious board members want to be more engaged in anticipating the future, decoding the external environment, and translating their knowledge operationally. How can they implement their concerns?

What isn't being asked in the boardroom is: Are we the right type of board for this organization in these times? As complexity increases we see early signs of something bigger—the emerging "must do" or mandatory transformation of fiduciary boards' identity, purpose and culture to meet 21st century challenges and opportunities. Something more substantive is needed. Our model focuses on transformation.

Begin to Think of Yourself as a Mindful Board Member

In the early 1970's, Robert Greenleaf, founder of the modern servant leadership movement, anticipated that institutions would fail and American democracy would decline because of a failure of good decision-making on the part of people entrusted to sustain our institutions. Their failure is not due to ineptness but "the failure of those endowed with intelligence, values, training, judgment, and experience" to accept with deep commitment "the obligations to serve the public interest with distinction." Exceptional service can be the standard that you hold for yourself as you use your talents and skills and engage your spirit in the work of the board. That same standard may be something you propose and bring into the consciousness of other board members.

"Mindful board member" is our term reflecting the mindset, capabilities, and actions of board members who are practicing Conscious Governance. The power of the person engaged as a mindful board member is an expanded energy and spirit that enliven not only her life and work of governance but also the relationships and work of the board. She is more aware of how to make a personal contribution and how the mission of the organization connects to personal purpose, so that board work becomes meaningful, not just convenient or opportunistic. Mindfulness generates power to see and act "to serve the public interest with distinction."

Such personal power requires humility and self-awareness. Being a mindful board member requires exquisite attention to self and others. It means listening inwardly and outwardly at many levels. It means being fully present in the meetings. The mindful board member has chosen to join a board on behalf of self, the enterprise and the society at large.

The mindful board member sees himself as both an independent voice and as a member of a community. This is the board member whose role identity embraces more than auditing the organization, carrying the ambassador flag, or approving a strategic plan. Rather, this person identifies with and practices:

1. Assuring all fiduciary responsibilities are met and done well.

2. Being a member of a working group savvy about operations.

3. Serving as one among many stewards of the strategic future of the organization.

4. Being an engaged member of a community that anticipates and monitors the impact of the enterprise on society and the planet.

Ideally, the mindful board member is one of many such members on a board. The synergy from a mindful board is inspiring. However, if you find yourself alone, begin building a small group of mindful members using the model, disciplines, and tools of Conscious Governance.

Take a First Look at the Path to the Mindful Board

Conscious Governance is a developmental model with four stages. The path to the Mindful Board involves building foundational disciplines, and using tools and strategies that propel you and the board forward.

The Continuum of Conscious Governance

Consent Board ➜ Working Board ➜ Strategic Board ➜ Mindful Board

The Boardroom—6 Tools

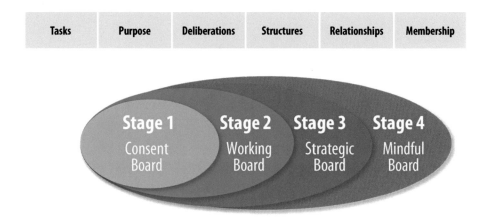

| Tasks | Purpose | Deliberations | Structures | Relationships | Membership |

Stage 1 Consent Board | **Stage 2** Working Board | **Stage 3** Strategic Board | **Stage 4** Mindful Board

Board Members and Officers—6 Disciplines

| Self-Awareness | Trustworthiness | Reflection | Expanded Consciousness | Fearless Engagement | Leadership by the Group |

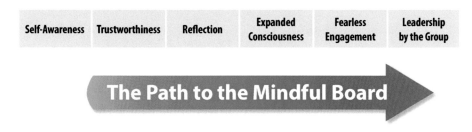

The Path to the Mindful Board

How to Talk About the Mindful Board
and Conscious Governance

Excitement about a new concept can be hard to communicate—finding the right words the first time you explain new ideas can make anyone feel muddy-tongued. Sometimes a script would help. Here is a way to talk with a colleague about breaking the constraints on the board where you lead or serve. If you're not sure whether you want to move toward Conscious Governance, these brief comments may be part of your dialogue with yourself.

What's the big idea?

"I'm thinking that it's time for us to re-evaluate our governance model in light of global changes. The dynamics are different in the 21st century, and the scope of a board's work is widening. I'm reading about becoming a Mindful Board, and I think we could shift our board in that direction."

Why do it?

"To become a Mindful Board means moving beyond just rubber-stamping the executive's plans. I can see how it opens up an exciting space where even one mindful board member can lead the full board to a deeper understanding of board service and more mindful impact of the whole enterprise on the community and the world."

What would we need to know?

"Think about how developmental psychologists have identified the stages of growth that children go through as they move toward adulthood. Think about how businesses move through developmental stages from start-up to maturity. A board can move through its own developmental stages as well. It turns out there are four distinct stages and several tools for moving from one to the next."

Where could we go with this?

"The overall goal is Conscious Governance. It is a way of making decisions as a board that is mindful of our impact on the enterprise and on the world beyond it. Conscious Governance could enrich

- our own experience of serving the public interest,

- how the enterprise fulfills its mission,

• and the impact of the enterprise on the planet.

I am thinking about how this will strengthen me as a board member."

Welcome to Prescient: A Tale of Transformation

We illuminate the dynamics of Conscious Governance through the story of Prescient, a fictional organization we created based on our work and experiences with governing boards.[2] Throughout the book, you'll read an update about what's happening at Prescient and see what we think the events reveal.

This method frees us to describe the human side of the process, which is often difficult to do when sharing real-life case studies. We begin here at a point in Prescient's history when board members and the CEO face critical challenges.

Something is Going Wrong at Prescient

It was time once again for the 3 to 5 year plan. Jim, CEO of Prescient, came into the board meeting with a draft. His tone and the style of the draft made it clear there was no place for input by the whole board. It was, in his mind, simple and easy to approve. "It's a done deal," he whispers to Marc, the board chair. Marc had given input to the CEO prior to the meeting—a fact he shared with the board. Similar to past plans presented by Jim and his team, this was an operational plan with little strategy and significant emphasis on short-term actions. Jim stuck to this approach in spite of recent articles in the *New York Times* and the *Financial Times* about Prescient's industry which suggested the strategy and operating model must change to keep up with competitors.

Sean, the board's newest and "wild card" member was the first to speak following Jim's presentation. He ignored the non-verbal cues from Marc and boldly asserted his concerns about the external environment and the plan in general. "We need a real strategy." He kept going, pressing his point about indicators that Prescient was falling behind and could be in big trouble if the CEO and board don't act soon.

George, an experienced and mindful board member, spoke next. He expressed confusion about why there was no recognition of the changing customer base in the plan as presented. He suggests that the purpose of the organization may be shifting or might need to shift to something new. George points to data brought into the meeting by Zach, the senior vice president of marketing, which indicated customers were somewhat dissatisfied. Some board members looked uncomfortable, others confused, and still others intrigued. Marc nods

---

[2]The story of Prescient is a work of fiction. Names, characters, the organization, events and incidents are either the products of the authors' imagination or used in a fictitious manner. Any resemblance to actual persons, living or dead, an actual organization, or actual events is purely coincidental.

to George but did not probe or ask him to explain his comments further. No one asked George to elaborate.

Discussion ensued about whether to approve the plan, and questions about customers, market share, and strategy started to pop. Sean pressed hard, arguing that the board cannot approve the plan until the board has more information about customers beyond what they have received to date. He wants to know how the customer data impacted enterprise performance. Suzanne, who was clearly edgy, reminds everyone the plan belongs to Jim and she felt the board was overstepping its role, "Besides, spending too much time on strategy when there is immediate action needed is wasteful." This ping-pong moment in the boardroom continued for nearly an hour.

Right at the moment when Suzanne, always impatient with process, seemed ready to leap out of her seat, Marc lowers the gavel and brought the discussion to a close. Marc puts off the vote to the next meeting and tells Jim to keep working on it. Jim was stunned. He left the boardroom shaken and disappears quickly into his office. Kim, Prescient's CFO, had sat quietly throughout the meeting. She stared after him in disbelief.

What we see in this first installment of the Prescient story

Notice in this first installment how a few board members express growing awareness of shifts in the industry and the pressures on Prescient. Notice also that other members seem unaware or unpersuaded that they belong in the arena of strategy. How many times have you seen this dynamic in a board or team? The question is whether the board will continue to press Marc and Jim or take a "wait and see" approach. What happens with the strategic plan will be important; however, as you will see, the plan will not be enough for Prescient.

Invitation

Practice builds competence. Conscious Governance can start with a significant decision by the board that fundamentally alters the organization's identity, operations, or presence in its markets. Boards that learn how to deliberate and discern together with executives develop capabilities they can call on when the next profound situation arises.

From our Case Files:

Three key decisions carried a healthcare board through their 10-year journey toward Mindful Board. The **first** decision was to integrate two systems reluctant to consolidate their operations and assets. They insisted they could not use "acquisition" or "merger" to describe the transaction because of political and cultural realities. Deliberations persisted for two years before both systems' boards could endorse the integration and totally new brand name. From that lengthy and involved process, the new board expanded its sensitivity to and understanding of the complexities of their industry. A few years later, a board member suggested a strategic change in their growth strategy that focused primarily on the metropolitan area. Their **second** decision has resulted in 19 facilities statewide. Their wide footprint across the state precipitated the **third** and profound decision to rebrand their organization, bringing back the former name of one of the entities—an impossibility 10 years earlier.

The current board and officer group have learned how to make weighty decisions mindfully with a formal process. To begin each board meeting, they have a "Connect to Purpose" moment to remind them of the organization's impact on the people they serve. When confronted with a "profound decision," the Values and Ethics Committee of the board convenes a group of citizens and members of the system for discernment on the question posed by the decision. The committee comes to the full board with a recommendation for action on the matter. Finally, the board is constantly looking at technology and other trends in their industry and considering implications long before state or federal regulations mandate action. They are conscious of their governance responsibilities to the past, present, and future of the organization.

In Chapter 2 you will walk the Path of Conscious Governance and get a strong impression of each of the four types of boards: Consent, Working, Strategic, and Mindful. Having walked this path many times with board members, we're eager for you to discover what might be possible for your own board. We invite you to join us on the journey.

Chapter 2

Where on the Path is My Board?

Effort and courage are not enough without purpose and direction.

— John F. Kennedy, Raleigh, NC on September 17, 1960

So here we are, governing in a world fraught with uncertainty, rapidly increasing global connectedness and competitiveness, greater interdependence across all sectors of our society, and an explosion of information and knowledge. This is not news. What is new is that we are better positioned than our predecessors to see and grasp the far-reaching consequences of our decisions for our organizations and society.

Boards exist to guide or steer the organization. We are being asked to lead in ways that nothing else in our lives has prepared us for, and yet we still dive in. How can we see our way forward? Will we know when we need to change?

From Our Case Files:

The chairman of a social services board struggled with what he saw as the future impact of technology on the work of the organization. He was also keenly aware that the board consisted mostly of friends of the CEO who had resisted adoption of technology advances and some human resources best practices for the last few years. The CEO assured the board that "our business is high touch." Not only did the chair see the need for a new CEO; he also needed more future-thinking board members. From his perspective and that of a couple of aligned board members, both the organization and the board were in crisis. He took action first to repopulate the board.

Explore the Map of Conscious Governance

You have discerned by now becoming a Mindful Board through Conscious Governance isn't a one-step process—it's a journey. At this point, a map of the territory may be useful.

Conscious Governance is the territory. It is the board's practice of governance for the benefit of the organization and all those affected by its activities. Several models of governance exist among for-profit and non-profit boards. The transformation of purpose and identity in tandem with the transformation of practice distinguishes Conscious Governance from other models. Self-awareness and reflection are essential capabilities for a board to determine their exact location in the territory.

We have identified four developmental stages in the Conscious Governance territory. Notice that the stages are nested within each other to reflect the nature of the journey.

As you read about the four stages, you will see distinctions in what matters to board members and senior officers at each stage as consciousness expands. You will see how leadership shifts from being owned and practiced by a few to a responsibility of the whole group guided by a few. And, you will see how the presence of mindful board members impacts how the board engages with the enterprise and the decisions brought before it.

Most importantly, when a board transforms from one stage to the next, it takes with *it the skills and capabilities of the previous stage.* The effect is cumulative. The result is astounding.

> **When a board transforms from one stage to the next it takes with it the skills and capabilities of the previous stage.**

You will read all about the disciplines of Conscious Governance and the tools at hand to lead the transformation in Chapters 3 and 4.

Right now, get the lay of the territory and the four stages.

The Continuum of Conscious Governance

Consent Board ➔ Working Board ➔ Strategic Board ➔ Mindful Board

The Boardroom—6 Tools

Tasks	Purpose	Deliberations	Structures	Relationships	Membership

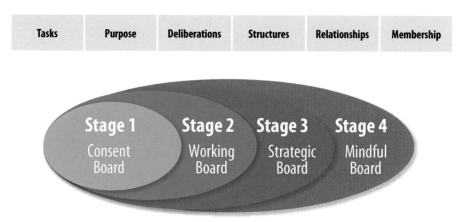

Board Members and Officers—6 Disciplines

Self-Awareness	Trustworthiness	Reflection	Expanded Consciousness	Fearless Engagement	Leadership by the Group

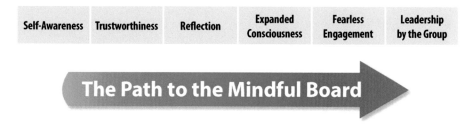

Walk Down the Path—Where is your board?

As you read, ask yourself:

- Where is your board on the path of Conscious Governance?

- Where do you think your board needs to be on the continuum?

Stage 1:
Consent Board—Defined by its Limits

Pre-Sarbanes-Oxley… 'Ceremonial' boards…existed only to perform their duties perfunctorily. …These boards perfunctorily performed a compliance role. Many directors served for the prestige and rarely spoke among themselves without the CEO present. They made sure to fulfill their explicit obligations, including attending the required board meetings and rubber-stamping resolutions proposed by management. …Most readers will recall a few boards that fit this description at some point in time. Hopefully, it doesn't sound like any boards on which they now serve, though these boards still exist.

— Ram Charan, *Boards that Deliver*

Observe the Consent Board at Work

The *Consent Board* is defined by its limits. Core fiduciary and mission oversight functions are central to the Consent Board's purpose. Its primary tasks center on supporting the CEO's initiatives and leadership. Structures (for example, policies, practices, committees, the decision-making model, membership rules, group norms, and leadership) are highly bounded in the Consent Board. The board chair and CEO own the board's tasks, structures and deliberations. Agendas move quickly through decision-making because no item for deliberation is brought to the full board without prior vetting by the chair and CEO and a few key members. Debate and dissent are generally frowned on during meetings; deliberations are expected to move relatively quickly and smoothly in keeping with the "no surprises" rule.

> The Consent Board has been described by others as a ceremonial board or "rubber stamp board" or patronage board. We use the term Consent Board to highlight specific characteristics.

The primacy of legal fiduciary responsibilities and support of CEO directives are at the heart of the Consent Board. Effective Consent Board members are financially savvy and trust the information provided to them by the CEO and board chair. Relationships among board members have social roots and multiple business connections. Individualism is highly valued. The board chair and CEO together manage the boundaries with high firewalls between the board and internal operations and between the board and external constituencies.

The strength of the Consent Board is consciousness of fiduciary requirements and rigorous attention to compliance with those responsibilities—especially in a post-Sarbanes-Oxley world. The weakness is its limited scope, with very little value placed on looking outward, and no tolerance for leadership by the group.

The Consent Board has been the traditional mindset for how a board should perform. Imagine breaking out from that model to a new identity in which attention expands, shared responsibility extends, and the importance of everyone's contribution comes into focus. The commitment to transform from Consent Board to the next requires significant discontent and courage.

Recognize Primary Assumptions and Operating Principles

The unique attributes of a Consent Board will vary depending on the specific organization, community, business context, and industry—as is the case at each stage. There are, however, primary assumptions and operating principles that consistently characterize a Consent Board. Life on a Consent Board looks like this:

Power means

- The board's primary task is to support and uphold the recommendations of the chief executive.

- The chief executive will manage the information flow to the board through the board chair.

- The power to determine right action for the enterprise lies first with the chief executive, second with the board chair, and third with the board.

- There is a hands off rule in the deliberations. Members should meet their fiduciary responsibilities and mind the boundaries. Questions that probe into management practices are deemed micro-managing and not appropriate.

Deliberations are guarded because

- Dissent and disagreement are not generally expressed during the meeting— this happens outside of the boardroom. It is important not to derail the consent agenda or deliberations leading up to the unanimous vote. The board may be engaged as a sounding board on specific issues, but conversation remains limited.

- The focus in meetings is on majority opinion, not on incorporating divergent views or interpretation of facts by individual board members. What might be termed "process" is considered not a good use of the board's time because the facts and conclusions have been presented by those with the greatest expertise—the CEO and/or his/her designee?

Individualism is valued because

- The intellectual, social and emotional life of the board resides somewhere outside of the board room, but can be accommodated before or after a meeting with golf outings, dinners, and community events.

- When board members show up for meetings, they come as individuals, not as members of a cohesive deliberating group. In fact, their most important attributes are their reputation and/or capacity for philanthropy (in the case of non-profits) that can enhance the credibility of the board and attractiveness of the organization.

Fences are clearly marked since

- Conscious Governance at this stage focuses only on what is at hand and is bounded by the board's interpretation of their fiduciary responsibilities. This can be done quite exquisitely, as long as it is done within the spoken and unspoken rules.

- Interactions between board and officers are formal. Presentations with slides dominate communication from officers.

How the Mindful Board Member Engages with a Consent Board

- Practicing the disciplines of reflection and self-awareness is a private matter for individuals and not valued as a group skill or contributing to effective governance. One or two elders may take on the tasks of making members aware of their thinking and reflecting on the organization's expanded impact by using powerful questions. They are, however, careful not to override or embarrass the CEO or board chair in meetings.

- The board chair and CEO lead the board. Leadership from the group is considered impossible, impractical and unrealistic. Any wise counsel by a mindful board member happens outside of meetings.

- Group development may be embraced if it is initiated by the CEO and/or board chair and is focused on specific issues or topics only. The mindful board member finds others who will support a change in the way the board operates before going public with the idea.

If the Consent Board Ignores Signs of a Changing Reality

When significant changes occur in the external and/or internal contexts of the organization due to an event (a shift in the industry trends, the Great Recession, or a new federal regulations, for example), the Consent Board can cease to be effective.

"It is unfortunate when a board is incapable of organizing itself to make critical decisions that will be held in public scrutiny. My current board does not have this capacity. They don't know enough to trust themselves. They're waiting for me to tell them what they should do."

— Interim CEO

What is at risk if your Consent Board ignores the external context or operational reality changes? One risk is dependency on the CEO and board chair for "answers" during times of change, crisis, growth, or uncertainty, limiting the potential responses to their experiences. Board members may defer to the executive committee for key decisions and lose engagement of the full board. They may have inadequate resources for making the best decision if they are dependent on the chief executive and officers for providing the best available information for the board's deliberations.

When internal and external contexts dramatically change, the Consent Board may not adequately review business strategy and general direction. The board's time frame tends to be current performance and the immediate past. If their perspective is limited to functions being impacted most by the changing contexts, patterns across the enterprise may be missed, which can be dangerous to the well-being of the enterprise. Narrow perspectives endanger how the organization interacts with key constituent groups, the community, stakeholders/shareholders, and investors.

Changing contexts require robust deliberations. Tapping the talents, wisdom and voices in the room can be lost when pressures increase on the Consent Board. Wisdom that could elevate the context intelligence of the board is missed. Avoidance of in-depth dialogue makes it difficult to retain talented board members who want their time spent to be worthwhile.

The Consent Board puts its purpose of fulfilling basic fiduciary responsibilities at risk by ignoring the need for transformation and continuing to do governance as usual.

Know When to Move Beyond Consent Board

Consent Board capabilities and functions never go away. A board should always be able to exercise these capabilities and perform all fiduciary responsibilities. A board may choose to go into "Consent Board mode" when the work or topic requires it at any point in time. Boards at later stages are able to use these capabilities to approve matters that senior leaders or committees have thoroughly vetted and recommended. Consent work improves efficiency of boards so they can engage complex or strategic issues in plenary sessions.

An array of drivers or pressures can signal the need to move to a new stage of Conscious Governance. Contextual changes may demand that all board members become more accountable and involved. The CEO and/or senior officers may find the business model dramatically changing, requiring board members to engage differently. The impetus to change may come from board members who feel uneasy with their limited role and want to head off "surprises."

If You Choose to Stay a Consent Board

Be conscious of the choice. The constraints of the Consent Board model arise from

- the limits of knowledge about internal operations,

- a board's deference to the CEO's and senior officers' exclusive strategic view of the enterprise, and

- board practices that limit deep conversation and reflection.

These constraints serve the board and organization well when appropriate. They can also restrict vital conversations that can unintentionally harm the enterprise over time.

Is your board at the Consent Board stage? If so, you may be bound by an invisible straightjacket. Wouldn't you like to know how to take it off?

Stage 2:
Working Board—Connects the Parts

Boards are vulnerable to problems of purpose both in their official and their unofficial work. As a result, it is not just trustee satisfaction that is at risk but also effective governing.

— Chait, Ryan and Taylor, *Governance as Leadership*

Observe the Working Board at Work

The *Working Board* brings forward into its new identity all the same fiduciary oversight capabilities and expands their understanding of operational effectiveness (for example, quality, safety, and employee engagement) and the overall impact on enterprise performance. The Working Board maintains its attention on the system's operational effectiveness, and connects and compares the internal operations to performance standards in the external industry.

Structures are somewhat less rigid. In particular, committees take on an expanded role of managing the board's attention on their area of focus, be that governance, product quality and safety, or talent management. Committee meetings allow Working Board members to be more engaged in discussions and comfortable with debate during deliberations. They hold a greater sense of shared responsibility for board performance as they practice leadership by the group.

The profile of membership expands as people from outside the social network are included. Members are recruited for their expertise. The tone shifts from closed club to colleagueship. Being a mindful board member is a welcomed and valued role even if there are only a few practitioners. The relationship among the board chair, CEO and board is still formal at this stage. As the board builds its understanding of operational effectiveness there is a heightened sensitivity among the CEO and officers to the risk of "micro-managing" or "micro-governing."

The Working Board's strengths are capitalizing on the expertise of members, better understanding of how the organization achieves its goals, and their ability to connect operational issues to strategic goals. Their primary weaknesses are getting too far into operational details and reluctance to leave familiar territory to explore strategic imperatives fraught with ambiguity and risk. Some board members may push to return to the perceived simplicity of the Consent Board.

Recognize the Primary Assumptions and Operating Principles

Life on the Working Board is distinguished by a new set of characteristics.

- Power is experienced differently.

- Members understand key operational and strategic issues linked to enterprise success.

- The board chair's role is that of integrator, relationship manager, facilitator and protector of the "secure space" for deliberations.

- The chief executive and senior leaders are treated as working partners and mutually responsible for the organization's long-term health.

Dissent is valued

- Discussions, debate and discernment are critical and valued elements of deliberations. Most robust conversations occur in committee meetings.

- Dissent, when civil and thoughtful, is viewed as vital to effective decision-making. People are less likely to be coerced into a unanimous vote.

Individualism gives way to group identity

- Maximum engagement of board members is valued as key to board performance.

- Relationships are complex because there is greater engagement, vulnerability or exposure and trust; relationships are a primary factor in board performance.

- Board members are able to make decisions as a group because of the work done by their colleagues in committees.

Fences and boundaries adapt

- Directors rely more on committee insights and recommendations and have less dependence on management and staff for information and understanding. Lower fire walls between board and staff make critical data accessible.

- If warranted, the board (not just the chair) may request and/or seek third party data or opinions to secure the future of the organization.

How the Mindful Board Member Engages with the Working Board

Mindful board members are welcomed and appreciated though not proactively sought after.

- Reflection, as a group practice, increases at this stage but is usually limited to committee discussions and dialogue. When mindful members demonstrate this capability it is generally valued, though sometimes there are awkward moments as a board chair or board colleague struggles with knowing how to proceed when insights or observations pull the deliberations into new territory.

- Leadership by the group is expanding, particularly in committees. There is a greater sense of mutual responsibility for assuring the committee is focused on the right work in the best way possible. In full or plenary board meetings there is still dependency on the chair and CEO and members continue to be careful not to override or undermine the formal authority.

- The mindful board member engages in dialogue about the internal and external contexts in a more dynamic way to stimulate broader thinking. The board becomes more conscious of the organization's impact and potential.

If the Working Board Ignores Signs of a Changing Reality

What is at risk if your board ignores the external context or operational reality changes? Over time, committees and the board can end up focusing too narrowly on a familiar set of topics, losing the capability to explore the unknown territory of long-term strategy. In the worst case, senior management feels they have to "manage" the board to get them "out of the weeds," resulting in blurred boundaries and eroding trust.

The board will be unable to guide or steer the long-term direction for the organization. If the Working Board continues to operate within committee silos, they will not see the organization as a system within a larger system. Their perspective will be fragmented and short-term. Trustees may avoid hard questions about the 5-10 year strategy and direction. Or, in the worst case scenario, the board could ratify management actions without rigorous discussion and negative consequences occur. This dynamic comes, in part, from a fear of damaging group harmony and closer relationships, which ironically can be as damaging as micromanaging. There is a risk that board members who are good strategic thinkers and innovators become bored or dissatisfied with committee work focused on operations and fiduciary oversight. They believe their skills and talents are not put to use and the work is less meaningful.

Senior staff will become responsible for interpreting changing contexts as they see it and providing committees with information about finances, operations, personnel and related matters. Executives can begin to dominate board and committee meeting agendas, content and conversations through the control of information and conversation over time. The board may inadvertently slide back into a Consent Board.

Officers may be de-motivated by what they perceive as micromanaging if your board is a skillful Working Board. Officers can feel the board is always second-guessing their well thought-out operational decisions. Talented officers may leave for more autonomy. The board/officer relationship can become strained as a result. The chairperson and CEO must monitor board and officer job satisfaction.

A Working Board may struggle developing its "own mind" separate from management's. To mitigate this risk, the governance committee can identify a learning agenda from the annual board evaluation and assure there is adequate time on agendas for board-only conversation. The risks mean the chairperson needs to deftly navigate independence from management.

Finally, the collegial culture is often fun and engaging, allowing complacency and oversight sloppiness to creep in. Not challenging the strategy, vision and mission routinely will put the organization's long-term sustainability and success at risk. There is a self-satisfying quality of Working Board life—why look beyond the 1-3 year horizon if you don't have to?

Know When to Move Beyond Working Board

The Working Board uses the competencies of the Consent Board (fiduciary oversight) with greater awareness and mastery as it integrates the new competencies focused on the operational and short-term strategic health of the enterprise. When is this not enough?

When the strategic plan becomes an annual exercise instead of a rigorous effort to bridge internal and external realities, it is time to transform into a Strategic Board. When board members find themselves frustrated with enterprise strategy and results, it may be time to move to strategic governing. If the CEO has missed business requirements and the board tries to provide the necessary strategic direction, it is time to transform.

External forces can drive the move beyond a Working Board. When disruption from downward shifts in business performance threatens to derail the chief executive and the organization, the chairperson may call for a broader focus of governance. "Game changers"—significant disruptions or revolutionary changes—dictate a need for strategic focus in partnership with officers.

If You Choose to Stay a Working Board

The Working Board is a great asset to a CEO in the midst of redesigning the business model, starting a new business line or product, or making significant changes to culture in the interest of fulfilling organizational goals and aspirations. The constraints of the Working Board arise from the board's choices to develop a deeper knowledge and understanding of the inner workings of the enterprise, which limit challenging dialogue about broader, long-term strategy.

The Working Board is usually competent in moving back and forth between Consent Board fiduciary responsibilities and attention to critical internal operations. The same board may struggle to respond when a customer, competitor, vendor or regulator creates a strategic issue in the marketplace. The board's internal focus limits their perception and response time to external shifts in the economy, industry and marketplace. One solution is to add a Strategic Planning Committee to manage the board's attention when appropriate. They remain a Working Board.

Is your board at the Working Board stage? How are the constraints showing up on your board? How can you loosen or break away from the strong constraints?

Stage 3:
Strategic Board—Go Beyond the Annual Report

Boards have to maintain a delicate balance in their relationship with management. They must be challenging and critical on the one hand and supportive on the other. They have to sustain an open and candid flow of communication in both directions. They must also seek external sources of understanding outside of management without offending management.

— Jay Lorsch, *The Future of Boards*

Observe the Strategic Board at Work

"Strategic board" can be explained different ways. Some authors and consultants describe this type of board as having an intense focus and involvement with strategic planning and monitoring. The CEO and officers still own strategy development and invite the board to participate as appropriate. Others describe this board as focusing their strategic attention on internal operational issues only. In either scenario, the board has not altered its core purpose and identity. A Consent Board or a Working Board can engage in strategic conversations or deliberations about the strategic plan to meet a specific need or crisis. The core purpose and identity of each, however, stays the same.

The *Strategic Board's* purpose and identity contain a resolute commitment to thinking in longer and broader terms for the organization. They look beyond the 3-5 year horizon while integrating insights from multiple sources into deliberations. The board understands the organization's wider reaches in its regional, national and international contexts. It takes a longer-term view of the organization's business success and considers its potential impact on the sector, industry or market. Seeking out wider and longer perspectives, it distinguishes itself through systems thinking—seeing both the interdependencies among the constituent parts as well as the whole organization in the context of larger systems. Board members hone their ability to ask higher-order questions that connect mundane transactions to long-term implications.

The board holds responsibility for the organization's long-term survivability. They partner with the CEO and senior officers to interpret data and external trends for immediate, mid-term and long-term effect on the organization's strategic direction. Their collective IQ goes up. The boundary between the board and officers is still intact—what changes is the conversation over the fence and subsequent action.

Strengths of a Strategic Board are their understanding of the organization's capability to respond to market conditions, their efficient execution of fiduciary responsibilities, their ability to think beyond the 3-5 year plan, and a willingness to work through divergent points of view to an eventual agreement on a robust strategic direction.

Recognize Primary Assumptions and Operating Principles

The Strategic Board's work balances the immediate with the long-term by focusing on the far horizon, fulfilling fiduciary responsibilities, overseeing the operational realities, and crafting strategic direction. Since members may serve over several senior officers' tenure, the Strategic Board keeps the organization's long-term best interests in the foreground at all times.

Life on the Strategic Board will include distinct characteristics beyond those of the Working Board.

Power is the group's intellectual capacity

- Board leadership pays attention to raising the collective intelligence of the board to amplify their capability to make robust decisions in the best interest of the next generation.

- The board engages with external experts to consider powerful, complex questions about the business.

- The board sees connections between the actions of the organization and the constantly changing contexts of the marketplace and industry.

- The board strives to fulfill the organization's mission and strategic direction over a substantial number of years.

Dialogue, discussion, debate and dissent are valued

- Deliberations use masterful inquiry and dialogue in consideration of facts, trends, issues and people. Ambiguity is expected, discomfort is okay, and patient perseverance leads to clarity.

- Dissent and conflict are important to navigate because they can lead to new insights.

- Board members challenge and collaborate with each other and senior officers as thought partners with a longer time horizon in view.

Diversity, collaboration and shared leadership expand

- Leadership is a shared responsibility with recognition that people who fill formal roles such as board chair and committee chairs are helpful as organizers, facilitators, historians, and most importantly, individuals who keep the relational space healthy and safe.

- CEO and officers lead strategic conversations and are valuable assets for leading the organization. By extension, succession planning is intentional and forward-thinking.

- Members with diverse backgrounds, expertise, professional experience and perspectives are proactively recruited because such diversity is central to strategic governance. This degree of diversity requires skillful practice of inclusion.

- Relationships grounded in trust and mutual respect are required if the board is to consider difficult strategic questions, puzzles and dilemmas.

Fences and boundaries are useful signposts

- To foresee, understand, or interpret trends, the board wisely utilizes third party expertise to challenge, inform and recommend.

- The board takes advantage of the diversity among board members and officers to draft a multi-dimensional map (financial, operational, social) of the organization in its markets.

- The CEO and officers are fully supported to implement the strategic direction and look for new horizons.

How the Mindful Board Member Engages with a Strategic Board

Mindful board members are recruited as well as developed for the Strategic Board.

- Two critical disciplines are increasingly important as the board becomes more comfortable with complexity and ambiguity. 1) "Reflection" is the ability to "think about our thinking around an issue" so we can give voice to differences and hear emerging insights. Assumptions and biases are tested. 2) Self-awareness allows us to understand contexts, think through our assertions, and sense how others are responding to our actions. Be a role model for personal reflection (Why do I think that?) and self-awareness (I can tell if I'm being effective in the group). Use facilitation techniques to help the group reflect and be aware of its own intentions for the organization.

- The mindful board member can point to changing contexts by sharing articles, reports and news that may stimulate questions and vibrant conversations. During deliberations, he/she can ask big, open-ended questions to push the board's mental boundary beyond the traditional 3-5 year horizon.

- Leadership by the group is embraced as the board moves to a new balcony of longer-term perspective and greater sensitivity to the impact of decisions. Formal roles are valued, but there is also an expectation that everyone knows when and how to "lead from any chair."

- Diversity deserves to be well managed. Notice interactions among board members and subgroups. A comprehensive evaluation of the board's performance can make sure no person or group is excluded and no particular agenda is pushed on other members. Board members must also honestly evaluate their effectiveness in seeing trends and anticipating changes.

- The mindful board member encourages others to contribute to the context intelligence of the board, and to expand his/her own consciousness about the interface between the organization and society. Participation can help build trustworthy relationships.

If the Strategic Board Ignores the Signs of a Changing Reality

A Strategic Board must be hyper-vigilant. Signs of a changing reality can appear inside the organization and out in the marketplace. What can happen if a Strategic Board ignores employee or customer satisfaction survey results or productivity losses? What if they miss seeing market context changes, a disruption in the industry, an extraordinary community event, or a shift in the social context of the enterprise?

The Strategic Board's primary risk is becoming hesitant to act quickly and failing to respond when immediate action is required. The result can be a failure to perform basic fiduciary responsibilities well or being blinded by their long-term bias to understanding pressures on the organization. Their concern for the greater good of society could cause delayed reaction. The organization is at a disadvantage.

There are risks to membership on a board with diverse points of view. Members can become angry or disillusioned when operational issues are, in their opinion, ignored, or there is a failure to see the critical connection between current state and long-term outcomes. Individuals who can see changing signs must have a plan for how to introduce the new data so others can see the pending risks and potential responses.

Senior officers can become frustrated with the board's inability to see what needs to be done and exercise their operational prerogatives to take action without full board support. In a different scenario, officers may have shifted too much of the burden of strategic thinking and planning to the board and blame the board for the consequences. As time passes, if officers believe they have been undermined, the talented people will resign.

Board leadership must carefully monitor the balance of responsibilities to ensure the fiduciary duties and operational management are done well. When out of balance, the board could lapse into a club atmosphere (similar to the Consent Board) if the focus is only on the organization's future and strategic direction.

Know When to Move Beyond Strategic Board

The Strategic Board's continuous scanning of the environment, understanding its contexts, and vigilance around the organization's contribution to its stakeholders creates the capability to evolve to the next stage, Mindful Board. As the Strategic Board's practice becomes firmly part of the board's culture, the way opens for an expanded purpose.

The board will know it is time to move to the fourth stage of Conscious Governance when the impact of the enterprise on a community, society and/or the planet becomes increasingly complex and weighty. When the social, economic, environmental footprint of the organization calls for renewed stewardship, it is time to transform yet again.

If You Choose to Stay a Strategic Board

You should consider constraints inherent in strategic governance. The Strategic Board becomes expert in seeing and acting on the relationship between the enterprise and its industry. This bounded view can miss the geopolitical-economic factors that can challenge the organization's sustainability and relevance. The Strategic Board's lofty perspective is, by its very nature, not a fully global perspective. If members go to their "balcony," where the view of the landscape below is limited to the industry or sector, they may miss internal operational or human resource trends capable of derailing the organization. As board members develop their expertise, they may not be able to address larger questions of often-ambiguous trends and harbingers of significant change.

Is your board at the Strategic Board stage? If so, how are the constraints manifesting themselves at this time? What matters most when considering releasing those constraints?

Stage 4:
Mindful Board—Decisions Reach Far and Wide

While the lines between for-profit and non-profit organizations have begun to blur, one simple fact remains clear: All corporations are chartered and given special privileges by the government in order to achieve the greater public good.

— Kent M. Keith, *Servant Leadership in the Boardroom*

The *Mindful Board* is the culmination of Conscious Governance. As a board advances on the pathway, members accumulate all the skills and capabilities from previous stages and expand the board's capacity to govern in complex systems. The Mindful Board is one that can deliberate, discern and act in a mindful way through critical decisions and episodes. Its purpose and internalized identity expand to include both the enterprise and attention to those impacted by the organization and its actions. Members think "beyond the walls of the organization" in time, space and intent and draw from a deep well of acquired capabilities—fiduciary oversight, operational leadership, context intelligence, systems thinking, and strategic thinking.

New business or service models demand new governance models. The board's core purpose and identity focus sharply on the broad impact of its governance across multiple systems. Here on the frontier of mindfulness we witness moments in boards' deliberations where the impact of the enterprise on the community, society and the planet is taken seriously and integrated into decision making. With the advent of new business models such as the benefit corporation, socially responsible corporations (CSR), services-on-demand APP-based companies, and redesigned public-private partnerships (such as in pharma-

> **With the advent of new business models such as the Benefit Corporation, socially responsible corporations, services-on-demand APP-based companies, and redesigned public-private partnerships the Mindful Board identity is becoming a business necessity.**

ceuticals, healthcare, and higher education) the Mindful Board identity is becoming a business necessity.

The Mindful Board considers guiding questions such as these: What is our understanding of what is right and fair for the enterprise when the issue does not have an easy answer? What is the board's transcendent social responsibility to employees, stakeholders/shareholders, and the community at large once we have made this decision? Do we know the risks and are we prepared to respond if unintended harm or bad outcomes are the result?

In discernment, mindful board members enrich the group's awareness of possibilities, consequences, and implications within a situation. Being "mindful" is not the same as being careful when faced with unusual or complex circumstances. Being mindful allows board members to stretch their perspective across systems and time to look for connections. People are expected to participate fully to increase the likelihood of a wiser decision by the whole board. Everyone understands themselves as stewards and leaders for the enterprise.

In the Mindful Board, structures are both adaptive and unifying. Committees are more ad hoc, with the exception of fiduciary standing committees, to respond to emerging trends and potential investment in new ideas, for example, with an eye toward the best far-ranging direction. On some regular schedule, the full board comes together as one unit to respectfully deliberate and make decisions in the best interest of the enterprise. The preferred time line for the enterprise may be in perpetuity or as long as customer demand is there. Deliberations are messy, inspiring and insightful.

Recognize Primary Assumptions and Operating Principles

Life on the Mindful Board moves the board's consciousness even further than in the previous three stages. Its work is to hold the creative tension of time (past, present, future) and space (inside the organization, its sector, and marketplace, the communities impacted directly and indirectly). The intention is to guide the organization's structure to fulfill its mission in perpetuity unless it is no longer relevant.

Power is the ability to anticipate

- Mindful governance carries a weighty responsibility that goes beyond the organization's survival; the enterprise attends to what is right and best for the constituents, community and society.
- The board purposefully pursues multiple perspectives when deliberating.

- Members look for emerging trends and sensitize others to the possibilities.

- The board enjoins the officers in envisioning a better organization.

Deliberations stretch members' thinking and awareness

- Discernment, the practice of divergent thinking to disentangle a complex issue, can lead to insightful decisions, though it may take a bit more time.

- There is value in accepting that the reality we see is only part of the reality. Mindful members must be committed to inviting in other perspectives and avoiding automatic responses. Everyone is right with her/his pieces of the truth, respecting that the full truth may never be fully known.

- Decisions made may not have full impact for ten or more years. The board must consider unintended consequences of a strategic plan, a crisis intervention, and/or the impact of ongoing operational decisions.

Board members act in community

- Board members pay attention in different ways depending on the subject matter and composition of the group; everyone stays aware of the flow of conversation—both what is spoken and unspoken.

- CEO and officers belong to the governance community by masterfully leading the business, maintaining strategic relationships for the organization, serving as thought partners with the board, and providing grounding for the Mindful Board.

- Individuals will be stretched beyond their personal limits in building a system for all stakeholders to see their potential. The board becomes a community of practitioners and the boardroom becomes a safe place to convene.

Fences and boundaries flex at times

- An organization consists of parts interacting to make the whole entity, which itself is only a part interacting as a part of another whole system. The Mindful Board appreciates and operates within this complexity.

- A Mindful Board will be a convener in the community, the industry, and relevant research and educational endeavors.

- Board members and officers appreciate differences between them in responsibilities, time space, and intent. They all develop their capacity to deal with dilemmas and unresolved tensions to prevent an important boundary from turning into a high wall.

How the Mindful Board Member Engages with the Mindful Board

- Everyone is expected to be a mindful board member. Some may be more facile or comfortable in spanning perspectives and seeing trends. Steve Jobs, co-founder of Apple, Inc., has been lauded as an exceptional visionary and inventor who could anticipate where technology was headed and create a solution before people knew they would need that solution. He used his intuition and instinct.

- Mindful board members engage their intuition and instinct with the other capabilities gathered along the Conscious Governance continuum.

- Practicalities of running the business are equally important. Members more experienced with Working or Strategic boards are expected to manage the board's attention in those areas when needed. Their perspective may reframe or simplify the situation.

- Mindful board members integrate differences into new patterns of thinking and acting.

- Mindful governance is more complex and messy. Reflection, rigorously testing one's thinking, remains critical as an individual and group discipline and practice. Self-awareness is part of the board culture and is expected between members and from senior officers. Trustworthy relationships contain the energy from the dynamic interactions. A mindful board member can lead the group from any chair when advancing the board's comprehension.

- The conversation and the collective thinking don't end when the meeting adjourns. Communication is facilitated among the governance community members to support learning and emerging ideas.

If the Mindful Board Ignores Signs of a Changing Reality

A complex system can experience change from many sources. The Mindful Board has to appreciate the difficulty in living with a 360-degree view. You can't possibly see all that is happening. When the board disconnects from current performance data, it risks being blind to signs of internal change. The board can inadvertently discount or disregard officers' recommendations on operating the business or competing effectively. The resulting rift can leave senior leaders resenting the lack of support as performance declines and board members being unaware of the urgent need to focus locally.

The Mindful Board risks paralysis when the multiple perspectives reach out too far beyond the known horizon. By constantly "star gazing," it can easily become overwhelmed by possibilities or ambiguity. The decision-making process could grind to a halt. The board has lost its bearings in its effort to grasp multiple contexts and the complex influences involved.

The pace and content of Mindful Board work can be taxing for its pragmatic, operational board members. If these valuable members leave, the board is untethered. Officers will have to refocus the board on the enterprise and its strategic needs.

When realized fully, the Mindful Board sees and acts from a commitment to both the organization and to the larger society. For this board, there is little doubt how the smallest action, connection, or decision links to a much larger system and beyond. Board members invite attention to what is the best, right action or process for the organization, believing those right actions can be catalysts for humanity, society, and in some cases the planet.

If You Choose to Stay a Mindful Board

Mindful Governance has some unique constraints for you to consider. The impact of an individual member is important at every stage of Conscious Governance. It is particularly important for the Mindful Board. Members with a particular interest may dominate while others disengage in meetings. Valuing individual expertise and maintaining a focused community of practitioners is a leadership challenge. Your experience may feel like leading a marching band toward the goal line while half the band turns at the 50-yard line.

One of the primary constraints in the Mindful Board model involves membership. Diversity is optimized on the Mindful Board to gather multiple intelligences on the board. Managing intellectual diversity can be intimidating. Potential members should be assessed for "fit" with the exceptional board. The intellectual flexibility required of Mindful Board members will limit who will fit, engage, and contribute meaningfully.

We interviewed executives who are familiar with both sides of the governance boundary as senior officers and board chairs/board leaders. They wondered, "How many members do you need who can think and work on a Mindful Board?" "Where do you find the individuals who can fit on a Mindful Board?" Each board has to answer these questions based on their specific situation. That said it is important to have more than one or two mindful board members to truly be a Mindful Board. Finding board members who will fit is the same process as with each of the previous stages.

Another constraint is leadership capabilities. All members need to be encouraged to easily move into the conversations and make their contribution. On the other hand, too many thought leaders around the table may limit and/or constrain governance at critical times.

Other constraints will appear as the Mindful Board becomes more common. The Mindful Board is only now emerging with new business models and the continued rapid evolution of all industries and sectors.

Is your board at the Mindful Board stage, or, is your board not yet at the Mindful Board stage but is demonstrating Mindful Board skills, values and capabilities? Regardless, how are the constraints manifesting themselves at this time? How well is your board integrating all four stages of Conscious Governance?

How to Talk About These Ideas

What's the big deal? A board is a board. Some are good and some are bad.

"There's more to it than good or bad. A board has to decide what type of board it needs to be to best serve the organization. There are four types of boards: Consent, Working, Strategic, and Mindful Boards. Each has its own identity and work. A board must match its identity with the needs of the organization."

Can you give me some examples?

"Well, the Consent board works best in a simple business that has a strong leader. Start-ups often have Consent Boards who are a sounding board for the founder. The founder still makes all the decisions. It's a limited model.

The Working Board suits a company that is growing and gaining market share. This board can focus on how the well the product or service is being produced, the quality of the workforce and their workplace, and how well the organization is meeting customer demand. This is an internal focus. You'll often see annual plans for improvement.

The Strategic Board works with the executives to take a longer look at the best path for the organization over the next 5-10 years. The organization is running well and competing in the market. Board members think "outside the walls" of the organization to include the industry and broader markets for inspiration. Taking the organization in a new direction might be a part of innovation and acquisition encouraged by the strategic-thinking board.

The Mindful Board is the culmination of all they've learned along the way. This board looks longer in time and farther in systems beyond the industry for what is right for the organization to thrive for many generations. They think about the operations of the business, the impact of the products or services, and how it competes in the industry. In addition, the Mindful Board considers the communities they impact, the socio-economic influence they have in these communities and how politics and different cultures shape their ability to make the world a better place.

There are four types of boards with four different identities. Each builds on the other to become a Mindful Board."

Can you show me an example of a Mindful Board?

"New business models have been created—a benefit corporation and socially responsible organization, for example. The primary goal of these organizations is not profit but 'doing good while doing well' in the world. Profits should be enough to be able to stay in business.

It makes sense that their boards must think differently. What is right and fair? How do we support employees, their communities and environments? How do our products make customers' lives better? Can we provide our products and services and do no harm?

The Mindful Board thinks and acts differently and relates to each other, officers, employees and stakeholders more inclusively. It takes time for a dedicated group of people to become a Mindful Board."

๑๛

Prescient Encounters Its Limits

The story continues. Notice the tensions rising as Marc wrestles with what is happening in the boardroom and with the CEO, Jim. These are early signs—little sprouts of growth—that Marc and others will want to nurture.

1 Month Later

Jim comes back to the board with a slightly modified draft. It has more marketing data gathered from focus groups held with nearby customers and others representing various constituencies. After the presentation, Marc thanks Jim for the work. Just as he is about to move forward with a vote, Sean raises a hand

and, without waiting to be recognized by the chair, starts to speak. "What does this plan mean about our future? Where are we going? Are we sustainable as is, or do we intend to be bought out? The data and the plan cause me to wonder exactly what we're doing. Should we consider a merger or acquisition based on what you've presented, Jim?"

Silence is followed quickly by the eruption of sidebar conversations around the room. Marc's usual good nature disappears as he turns to Sean, "It is not our job to micro-manage, Sean." Awkward silence fills the space. Marc looks sharply around the room and ends the session with, "We'll continue this discussion at our next board meeting. In the meantime, I'll meet with Jim."

Marc Reflects

The last exchange between Jim and the board troubles Marc. As he reflects on Prescient, he finds himself wondering if the board's support of Jim and the team, while well intended, is somehow off the mark. It is as if the discomfort of vocal board members is pushing Jim in some direction—one he does not quite grasp. Certainly Sean is asking good questions. He saw the looks of others as well. Robert, Harry and Todd were all visibly on edge after the last discussion of the plan. As his coffee cools, he thinks of George, who has left several messages of late. At some point, he must follow up. In the meantime, the marketing data and year-end results need the board's attention. Perhaps the board needs attention, Marc thought. For the moment, he pushes that elephant aside.

What we see in this installment

The external environment is putting significant pressure on Prescient and its board. Uncomfortable questions are starting to stir things up, and Marc's responsibilities as board chair are about to increase. You can see how the assumption that asking questions can be perceived as "micro-managing" could get in the way of good oversight if Prescient's board doesn't figure out how to engage the tough questions. Marc's thought that perhaps the board needs attention is going to be important to move beyond Consent Board.

Chapter 3

Dive Deeply into the Disciplines

For an innovation in human behavior, the components need to be seen as disciplines. By "discipline," I do not mean an "enforced order" or "means of punishment," but a body of theory and technique that must be studied and mastered to be put into practice. A discipline is a developmental path for acquiring certain skills and competencies. ...To practice a discipline is to be a lifelong learner.

— Peter Senge, *The Fifth Discipline*

Embrace the Disciplines of Conscious Governance

Conscious Governance is a developmental model with four stages. The practice of six disciplines will allow a board to move through the stages to become a Mindful Board.

A *discipline* is an area for *study* and *practice* that assumes life-long or continuous learning and development. To practice a discipline you assume there is always more to learn about both content and application; there is feedback from outside of yourself that guides how you exercise the discipline; and, your mastery will deepen over time as the context changes. A capability is the result of knowing *how* to use the knowledge and skills associated with a discipline to achieve a goal or carry out a task.

Conscious Governance requires these disciplines to become the Mindful Board:

- the individual disciplines of self-awareness, trustworthy relationships, and reflective practice developed by each individual as well as the board as a whole; and

- the collective disciplines of expanded consciousness, fearless engagement, and leadership by the group developed by each individual and board as a whole.

Living these disciplines is an artful practice. The "art" is the way you develop each discipline in a manner that reflects who you are as a person. The same applies to the board as group. The "discipline" of Conscious Governance embraces the intentional practice of the knowledge and skills associated with each discipline. As the board moves from one stage to the next, the board and its members practice the disciplines in the manner best for the enterprise at that moment.

Board Members and Officers—6 Disciplines

Self-Awareness	Trustworthiness	Reflection	Expanded Consciousness	Fearless Engagement	Leadership by the Group
Individual disciplines for board members and the board as a whole to develop and practice			Collective disciplines for individual board members and the board as whole to develop and practice		

Practice Self-awareness, Trustworthy Relationships and Reflection

Invite the Art and Discipline of Self-Awareness

Self-awareness begins by knowing who you are as you walk into the boardroom: your role on the board, your status on the board, your talents and expertise, and your opinions and ideas about the agenda. It means knowing the contribution you want to make by serving on the board. Members may believe that's easy and natural until they need self-awareness on four dimensions in the boardroom: self, board, officers and enterprise. Keeping your mind open and aware in each of these dimensions during presentations and deliberations isn't easy. Consider how these questions point to the importance of the discipline of self-awareness:

- How can any board member be effective without understanding her/his biases and assumptions as well as her/his role in the group?

- How can a board claim to be effective without being self-aware of its group capabilities and dynamics?

- How can a board govern consciously without a true partnership with the officers who will implement and lead directives from the board?

- How can the board make effective decisions without clear awareness of the institution's presence and performance in its market?

Self-awareness also means attuning yourself to context. How am I, in my role as board member, adjusting my interactions to fit the context, circumstances, issues and group norms? Individual board member comments can have an enormous impact during challenging conversations—especially when those comments invoke reflection on the situation. At their best, the self-aware board member's insightful comments about the situation at hand can stop the action long enough for board members to consider how to proceed.

The board as an intact group also needs self-awareness of the quality of its relationships, how it exerts power and authority, types of thinking it does well, topics that are nearly undiscussable, and how effective it is at guiding the organization by knowing its strengths and weaknesses. The board's awareness of the institution in its market is a form of context intelligence and requires attuning to how the organization performs relative to competitors, customers' needs and reputation in the community. The board practices collective self-awareness as it interacts with senior officers, constituents, external customers and stakeholders/shareholders. It expands its awareness by opening up flow of information and new insights.

The challenge of self-awareness is that often we think we are practicing it, but we may not get the feedback needed to see how we are really doing. Individuals and groups have blind spots in their perceptions. Individuals engage a coach to help them become aware and improve. A board benefits from skilled facilitation that offers direct feedback to the group and individuals. Feedback about individual and collective self-awareness can benefit the relationship between board and officers when building alignment around mission and strategic direction.

Engage in the Art and Discipline of Trustworthy Relationships

When faced with challenges and opportunities, individual board members who practice *self-awareness* and *trustworthy relationships* create openness and personal safety for the individual, group, and/or enterprise to uncover what is known and unknown. If the board hears from employees, customers, vendors, officers, special interest groups or regulators, the board is expected to respond. They must be able to test the facts, state perceptions and assumptions, and explore implications together. Board members need to know it is safe to talk openly. They need to trust the relationship with other board members.

Trustworthy relationships are grounded in compassion, humility, and respect. The quality of relationship we are describing does not just happen. Trustworthy relationships require a commitment to creating and nurturing them. Subgroups of like-minded members on a board, a natural social structure, can either heighten trust or put it at risk. A significant benefit of nurturing trustworthy relationships is the board's ability to act as a community where every individual board member and the board as a whole commit to engaging the toughest issues and deliberations without reproach or fear.

One board conversation that demands trustworthy relationships is evaluating executive performance and determining the executive's compensation. Another is dealing with a board member who does not see her or his conflict of interest. Such deliberations require confidentiality. Board members should be able to count on trustworthy relationships.

From our Case Files:

After intense deliberation, a board decided to get a second opinion from the organization's long-standing compensation consultant on the proposed increase in officers' salaries. This independent move was new for the board. It challenged the strength of the board's relationship with the officers and the tenured consulting firm. The board chair stayed self-aware and sought out feedback as the effort proceeded and incurred extra expenses. The board's relationships with officers withstood the new external pressure because the board chair frequently communicated with the CEO and key officers on the process. The results were a board more confident about relevant data and a stronger board-CEO relationship.

Value the Art and Discipline of Reflection

For centuries, "reflection" has been valued as a skill and discipline. *Reflection* has been a means to achieve insight and inspiration, and is useful in learning and developing expertise. Reflection as an art suspends disbelief and engages in "seeing" the world around us and our actions in it differently. As executives, practitioners and scholars, we reflect on our thinking, assumptions, and experiences to understand better what has occurred and what is happening. *As a discipline, reflection has become a hallmark of mature leadership*, as thought-leaders such as Jim Collins and Ron Heifetz remind us. The skill of reflection develops through dialogue enriched with questions that pull us out of our comfort zone and into discovery.

Reflection illuminates Conscious Governance. When individual board members learn and practice the discipline of reflection, they become good facilitators for critical conversations. When the board as a whole intentionally employs reflection as part of their repertoire,

> **The skill of reflection develops through dialogue enriched with questions that pull us out of our comfort zone and into discovery.**

they can clearly see the distinctions among the four types of boards and which type is best for their organization. Underlying processes and patterns become apparent to members and heighten understanding of a challenge or opportunity. The combination of individual and group reflection has an exponential impact on how the board deliberates and acts.

Reap the Rewards of Reflection + Self-Awareness + Trustworthy Relationships

When board members and the board as whole develop and incorporate the first three disciplines into the board's performance expectations, the way opens for three additional disciplines:

- Consciousness expands, and with it, the ability to do the tasks of governance and board transformation in a manner that serves the enterprise and society (expanded consciousness).

- The individual board member models and helps others to engage fearlessly in the most difficult discussions with extraordinary respect and attunement to others (fearless engagement).

- Leadership capabilities expand, power and authority is distributed, and the board, as a group, can lead (leadership by the group).

Cultivate the Repertoire of Disciplines

A board that gains mastery of the first three disciplines is an extraordinary board. Imagine energizing their governance practice by adding three more disciplines. A board can now draw on the energy, skills, talents, and individuality of all its members as it moves along the continuum toward the Mindful Board.

Encourage Your Own Expanded Consciousness

The concept of consciousness connects attention, relationship and meaning-making. *Expanded consciousness* attunes us to the world around us and within ourselves. It focuses us on our interactions with others in a given situation. It generates awareness of others as we participate in dialogue and decision-making. Consciousness regulates our willingness to seek a new perspective, a new meaning to data or a set of facts in a situation, or a new understanding about the emerging future. Consciousness increases our ability to observe self and others in a given moment, how we reflect on a particular situation, or how we transcend our current perspectives through our questions, relationships and insights.

There is a fundamental difference in the board's mindset and shared identity among members of a Consent, Working, Strategic or Mindful Board. As a board's consciousness or the board's "mind" develops, it expands its ability to perceive current and future forces at play and to work harmoniously with others. When a board moves along the continuum of Conscious Governance, consciousness develops, increasing the board's awareness of how it serves the enterprise.

In *The Fifth Discipline* Peter Senge describes this ultimate level of consciousness with the little-known word *metanoia*. "The word has a rich history. For the Greeks, it meant a fundamental shift or change, or more literally transcendence (*meta*—above and beyond) of mind (*noia* from the root *nous*)."[3] So we are striving for a consciousness that reaches beyond self for the purpose of accessing higher level insights and deeper understanding. Through this experience, "we reperceive the world and our relationship to it…we extend our capacity to create, to be a part of the generative process of life."[4]

When your mind shifts from a focus on self to the extraordinary nature of the moment and a sense of connection to everyone else and something beyond yourself, you are in a higher consciousness. When we grasp the complexity of a situation and can turn our frustration into freedom to create something new, we have discovered another level of consciousness.

---

[3]Senge, Peter (1990). The Fifth Discipline: The Art & Practice of The Learning Organization. Doubleday. p. 13
[4]Senge, Peter (1990). The Fifth Discipline: The Art & Practice of The Learning Organization. Doubleday. p. 14

Practice Fearless Engagement

Fearless engagement is not chaos or mayhem or egocentric diatribes released into the boardroom in a fit of frustration: it is the exact opposite. It does, however, require courage and the confidence to take risks from time to time.

The discipline of fearless engagement has distinct attributes: it can a) expand what we see; b) clarify reality(ies); and c) create the safe space for the conversations.

"Expand what we see" is about enlarging the view of a situation, an issue, the organization as a system, and/or the external context. This can occur through asking provocative questions that force the group out of complacency. It can include bringing in an article on a hot topic, inviting in an outside speaker, or offering new interpretations of data and outcomes. *Practicing fearless engagement* models openness to new information and perspectives for the tasks of governance. You can see how the disciplines self-awareness, trustworthy relationships, and reflection are so vitally important to maximizing the contribution of fearless engagement.

"Clarifying reality(ies)" does not mean getting to a specific endpoint. It means increasing awareness and acceptance of the complexity of any situation, issue or matter at hand. With fearless engagement, board members can challenge assumptions about "what is real" or "what is the truth" respectfully. Equally important is naming aloud what is not known, inaccessible to the group, or out of focus. Clarifying reality can prevent a board from tipping into the trap of false conflict. In the midst of the messiness or muddiness, taking time to disentangle the complex web of biases and emotions makes it possible to proceed.

To "create safe space," the mindful board member and others set the tone and model behaviors that make it possible to expand the view, ask difficult questions, and be open to new realities. Safe space in the boardroom allows members to have awkward or silent moments and express emotions such as hope, worry, anger, and confusion. You draw on the disciplines of self-awareness, trustworthy relationships, reflection and expanded consciousness when you, as a mindful board member, create safe space. "Safe space" does not mean "anything goes or an avoidance of upsetting emotions." Rather, it is the space to seek out and build shared understanding of the complexity that is woven into today's fabric of governance.

Trust Leadership by a Group

Everyone in the boardroom has a responsibility for leadership by the group. The discipline of *leadership by the group* does not undermine the formal leadership structure of the board or enterprise. As a discipline, it means building your knowledge and practice of leadership that draws out the best in every member and strengthens the board's capabilities. Recall the lesson of "two heads are better than one." Leadership by the group makes it possible for a board to rise to its highest level of performance in deliberations, relationships, and service to the enterprise and society.

By the time we have grown into early adulthood, most of us have experienced leadership *of* a group. We may have participated in group decision-making in various forms, most always under the guidance of an identified formal leader who was either presented to us or voted into the position. The leader often retained the right of final decision or guided the group to arrive at the desired result. Occasionally the leader would turn the decision over to the group and agree to support the outcome. Embedded in the group process was a natural hierarchical structure with rules (spoken and unspoken), procedures, and behaviors that told us we were not part of the leadership.

This was the primary model of group leadership mastered in the 20th century and is the one that most current board members expect in both non-profit and for-profit enterprises. Upon joining a board, we look around to find the formal and informal leaders, committee structure, basic processes, and approaches to decision-making. We expect the structures, the formal leaders, the various member roles, the board responsibilities, the ongoing tasks, and the goals to be clear. As we pull up to the table, literally and figuratively, we are ready to join a decision-making group very much like the ones we experienced in the past.

The heart of Conscious Governance is the imperative to lead as an integrated, high functioning *cohesive group with collective consciousness and shared purpose*. This type of leadership is not without its structures, formal leadership roles, and decision-making processes: quite the opposite. It demands greater individual and group self-awareness intentionality different from most of what we experience in our work and personal lives. Fearless engagement enlivens others to join in. Board members need skills to participate in productive conversation, constructive discourse, strategic thinking, scenario planning, financial analysis, and other critical work actions. They also need to know when shared leadership and individual readiness to lead is necessary.

How to Talk About These Ideas

The objective of this chapter is to surround you with the *six disciplines of Conscious Governance*. We present them in a particular order to offer logic to your learning agenda. You already practice some of these disciplines and we hope we've added some new dimensions. For the ones you're less familiar with, you have a starting point.

Disciplines. What a crazy word. What does that mean?

"Disciplines are the basic elements of Conscious Governance. If we want our board to improve its performance, we can start developing our practice of these six disciplines. Each discipline becomes an area for study and practice."

Okay. What are the six Disciplines?

"Three disciplines start with the individual: *self-awareness, reflection, and trustworthy relationships.* You and I can start there now to be better board members. When there are several members who are practicing these three, the entire group begins to see how they work and the benefits of practicing them. The board starts using the disciplines.

As the group gets better at thinking and acting together for the benefit of the organization and its stakeholders, the other three disciplines come into play nicely. These three are necessary to make the journey to the Mindful Board. *Expanded consciousness* is a commitment to being open to new perspectives and willing to accept that what we believe is true is only part of the picture. We will always have more to know and see. *Fearless engagement* is a value the board holds for each member. You must bring your talents, expertise, and views into the boardroom in service of exceptional governance. No hanging out on the sidelines. You won't always be right or convincing, but you are obligated to challenge the group's thinking and actions. Fearless engagement opens the way for *leadership by the group.* Strategic dialogues and insightful deliberations require everyone be fully engaged. Formal roles of board chair, committee chairs, and officers are more interdependent and adapt to the needs of the presenting situation."

Do you think we can do this on our board?

"I want to give it a try and become a better board member. I care about this organization's mission. If we get better as a board, we will help the organization fulfill that mission. That would be a great satisfaction for me."

How would we get our board members to take time to learn about the disciplines, let alone continuously study them? We try to keep our meeting tight.

"Two ways come to mind. We first have to introduce the model of Conscious Governance and find out where we think we are on that continuum. That's a half-day retreat. Once we have enough people who want to move to the next stage, we can decide where to start. We won't know the path to take until we get board members and key officers talking about it. That meeting will take all six disciplines to be successful!"

Prescient's Board on Retreat—
The Disciplines Mattered

The previous installment of Prescient's story brings us to a critical point. Dissatisfaction with the status quo is just starting to erupt among board members. Marc, the board chair, is unsettled by the reactions to the CEO's latest version of the strategic plan. George is emerging as a mindful board member during deliberations and in his conversations with Marc about the board and its relationship with Jim, the CEO. The situation is intensifying.

Look at What Has Occurred

After another series of difficult board meetings, tensions between board members and senior officers have intensified. Marc and George meet frequently to discuss the situation and how the board is responding to Jim's efforts to address the drop in market share. Marc finally agrees, though reluctantly at first, to scheduling a board retreat. The purpose, George reinforces several times, would be to focus on how the board is performing and interacting with Jim and each other.

When Marc presents the idea to the board he is surprised at how quickly the group agrees to the idea. He asks George to outline the purpose of the retreat and how it would work. George carefully explains the purpose is to get the board and Jim on the same page about the situation. This includes, he tells them, looking hard at how the board is conducting its business, expectations of each other at this time, and how to best move Prescient forward. He assures everyone that Jim would participate in the retreat. Marc asks George to take the lead.

George has laid the groundwork well ahead of time. A few weeks before the board meeting at which Marc proposed the retreat, George invited Sean to lunch.

"Sean, I need you to help me with something," George said over coffee. "You are raising great questions. I see how other board members are responding to you. You are getting conversations started we have never had before. Have you noticed, though, how when we get going and everyone is talking that we don't stop and ask ourselves, 'Are we thinking about the issues in the right way?' I want you to help me catch when the group needs to slow down and reflect on the conversation. I believe this will help Marc, Jim and the board."

Sean nodded, "I see your point. Particularly at the last meeting when Suzanne went ballistic over the data and I heard Robert, Harry and Todd all jump in at the same time. They ended up arguing with everyone. I lost track of what we were trying to figure out."

"Exactly my point," George added. "Thank you. You'll be a great help."

"And, George," Sean added, "I hope we can reassure Jim that challenging him does not mean we are unreliable. I hope he can trust us."

At the time George had lunch with Sean he was already pretty sure the retreat idea would be accepted. In addition to Sean, he has tested the idea with several other board members, as has Marc. At the board meeting just before the board retreat, George and Sean successfully intervene on two occasions. While the moments when the board stop and reflect on what is happening are not without their flaws, it becomes quickly evident the move has been well worth it. The group settles down and refines the questions floating around the room.

With Marc's support, George enlists Sean, Sophia and Jim to work with him on the retreat agenda and design.

Notice the disciplines in action

The individual disciplines of self-awareness, trustworthiness and reflection were all part of George's request of Sean and their subsequent actions. George and Sean have needed to take the lead with the concrete action of stopping the conversation and inviting the group to reflect. The board and Jim have needed to trust the "stop and reflect" action and they have needed to stay alert to how they are reacting in the moment as well.

The Morning Session Went Well

George is pleased with how the retreat is going. The retreat started off with a presentation from a local expert on trends in another industry that were directly and indirectly impacting Prescient's situation. This was followed by a combination of small group and whole board conversations about the implications for Prescient's operations and strategy.

During the morning break the buzz in the room is quite loud. Several board members speak to Marc about how their "brains hurt" from thinking about something so "wildly different" from what Prescient board conversations usually entail.

While some members are eager to jump to action steps, George and Marc convince everyone to hold off until later in the afternoon. "That way," Marc offers, "we will be better positioned to think about action steps in, hopefully, some new ways." As a result, by the time lunch comes around everyone is energized.

Notice a technique for shaking up the environment

One of the strategies for learning and applying the discipline of expanded consciousness is the use of outside speakers who challenge our beliefs and assumptions about a situation or the general status quo. It looks like using the outside expert has been a good idea for Prescient's board at this moment in time. Board members are "ready" to hear the ideas.

Join the Afternoon Session

The afternoon focuses on the board itself and how the board is partnering (or not) with Jim and his team. George and his design team had planned on guiding the group through a series of questions designed to get at what board members believe about the board's role and their relationship with CEO. As the discussion heats up, it becomes clear that not everyone believes in "partnership." "We hire the CEO and we must let the CEO be the CEO," Harry grumbles. It is as if Harry set off an alarm system.

Sophia steps into the conversation, "Harry, I appreciate what you are saying. Though, honestly, I think we have been absentee landlords at times. We have expected Jim to navigate this crazy economy without offering anything other than moral support. I believe we can—and must—figure out how to work together if Prescient is going to be around in 10 years."

After another twenty minutes of debate, George joins in. "It sounds to me that about half of us are comfortable with being more active partners with Jim and the other half of us aren't quite sure. It will probably help us figure out what we need to do differently if we apply what we're saying to the current situation." With Sean's help, they frame the question: What actions can the board take to partner with Jim that will make it easier for him to lead Prescient in partnership with us?

The energy in the room goes from concerned bordering on irritated to positive and curious. After another round of conversations a variety of ideas emerges. Harry smiles and offers a suggestion, "Let's make a list on the flip chart. Maybe even try to prioritize the ideas. Maybe that way we'll see what's realistic."

They create the list and the suggestion of forming an ad hoc strategic planning group pops up as #1. A small group of directors would work with Jim and members of his officer group to craft the most critical strategic imperatives. They would bring these ideas back to the full board for discussion and approval. Developing the operational plan to drive the imperatives would continue to rest with Jim.

They complete the prioritization and silence falls in the room. Marc leans forward in his seat, "I like this idea. How about if Jim and I talk about who might serve on this ad hoc group and I'll get back to you by the end of the week?" Just about everyone nods approval. After a few more moments, restlessness increases. It looks like George is about to declare a break when Suzanne raises her hand—a gesture no one has used all day. Before anyone acknowledges her request she poses her concern. Her tone is edgy and brittle.

"Jim, are you OK with this idea? I just hope we're not creating more bureaucracy or making life even more difficult for you." Everyone in the room turns in one smooth movement and looks at Suzanne—their faces reflecting a range of emotions and varying degrees of surprise. Jim sees the reaction.

"Suzanne, thank you for your question," Jim quickly replies. "It is certainly different from what we've done before, but I'm truly OK with this. I need your help. Prescient is at a crossroad."

The afternoon moves along. By the end time, it becomes clear to all present that this retreat is just the first of a series of serious conversations. Some members, like Harry and Robert, are not satisfied that enough was accomplished. Others express opposite opinions. Everyone agrees another retreat should be planned for a few months from now.

Look at Fearless Engagement in Action

Take note of the stunning effect of *fearless engagement*—both Harry and Sophia dared to speak up and others followed. *Leadership by the group is emerging.* The group's willingness to create a list of potential actions that would shift the partnership with Jim while being good stewards of the organization was a powerful move. It is possible the morning's session with the outside expert expanded consciousness enough to make new ideas easier to consider.

No one person appears to have dominated; rather, they expressed their leadership through clear understanding of what the ad hoc strategic planning group would do and not do. There is much more for this board to talk about and address. It is clear they have opened new windows into the industry and the organization. The amount of positive energy suggests readiness to consider how the board needs to change.

Stay tuned. There is more to come for Prescient.

Chapter 4

Open the Toolbox

Progress is impossible without change, and those who cannot change their minds cannot change anything.

— George Bernard Shaw

What resources do we have? What do we do?

You and your colleagues have an idea why your board needs to change and how they can practice governance differently. Before you begin the process of moving from one stage to the next, open the toolbox to see what resources you have.

Six tools are readily available to you. You don't have to buy them or seek them out. They are a normal part of your board's culture, but you will use them differently in each of the stages of Conscious Governance.

Get Ready to Do More than Tinkering on the Edges

When most of us think about developing a working group, we often think first about familiar techniques and strategies: facilitated dialogue, goal setting, team retreats and learning more about an issue from an expert. We

A complex journey demands diligent preparation. Familiarize yourself with the tools now.

have all experienced their usefulness. However, leading a group along the path of Conscious Governance from one stage to the next requires tools and techniques that generate transformational development. Our set of tools increases the likelihood of a successful journey for your board. These tools support the board's practice of the six disciplines. Of course, you may use other tools to build the board's capabilities in any one of the disciplines. We focus your attention on this tool set because it's available and effective.

A complex journey demands diligent preparation. Familiarize yourself with the tools now. When used singly, each is useful for incremental changes. We describe combinations of the tools that can accelerate each transition in Part 2.

The Continuum of Conscious Governance

Consent Board ➔ Working Board ➔ Strategic Board ➔ Mindful Board

The Boardroom—6 Tools

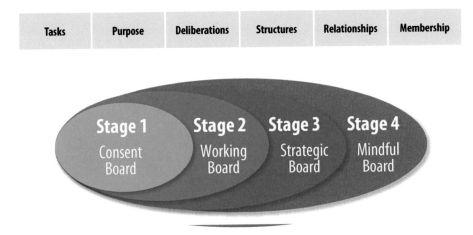

| Tasks | Purpose | Deliberations | Structures | Relationships | Membership |

Board Members and Officers—6 Disciplines

| Self-Awareness | Trustworthiness | Reflection | Expanded Consciousness | Fearless Engagement | Leadership by the Group |

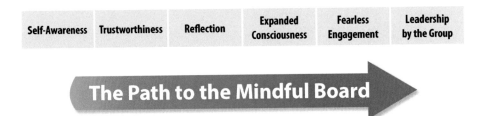

The Path to the Mindful Board

Tasks, Purpose, Deliberations, Structures, Relationships, and Membership

Six elements comprise the infrastructure of all governing boards and are critical to how the governance system operates: tasks, purpose, deliberations, structures, relationships and membership. Sometimes aspects of these elements are quite visible—they even have committees assigned to manage them! Other times what lies beneath the surface may not be immediately obvious. In either case, understanding the current state of this powerful infrastructure requires asking questions.

Tasks: What commands the board's focus and attention in meetings and outside conversations?

Purpose: Why does this board exist? What is the deep, abiding purpose or value of this board?

Deliberations: What best describes the quality of deliberations and decision-making?

Structures: What are the most influential structures and mental models? How is leadership, as a part of the board's culture, understood and enacted at this stage? How do practices and processes reflect what we believe about governance and leadership?

Relationships: What distinguishes the quality of relationships inside the board and between the board and senior leadership, customers, community leaders, regulators and other constituents?

Membership: What is important about membership (and being a member) at this stage? What are the criteria for selecting members?

These elements become the tools for *consciously* transforming a board.

Two cautions come with these tools. First, each of the six tools also transforms as you move from one stage to the next. For example, *deliberations* in the Consent Board are very different from deliberations in the Strategic Board. Membership changes from friends of the CEO on a Consent Board to talented colleagues in committees on a Working Board. In these examples, the tools of *deliberations and membership* are also transformed in the next phase. How you use the tools will change as the board moves along the continuum.

The second caution is you can't pick-and-choose one or two among the six tools to transform. To reach a new stage of Conscious Governance, you must engage *all of them*. The sequence is your decision; it may be obvious which one or two tools to use at the beginning to "flip the switch" and generate momentum. In Part 2 we offer some suggestions, but you will need to customize the approach. How long you focus on any tool varies based on the progress of the board. You can deploy these six tools in different ways and offer different degrees of leverage. But you must engage all six tools to fuel the board's transformation.

Expand the work of a board and you begin changing its purpose and its identity. ...A "simple request" initiates significant change.

You must custom design each transition to fit the board's readiness. You have to plan how the tools are used. Moving along the continuum towards the Mindful Board, the board (as a whole), individual members, and senior management can pay attention to all of these elements as indicators of progress.

The Conscious Governance Table of Tools for Transformation

Look at how the elements transform at each stage of Conscious Governance.

Core Elements	Consent Board	Working Board	Strategic Board	Mindful Board
Tasks	*Support CEO Initiatives*	*Understand Operations*	*Ensure Strategic Direction*	*Oversee Contribution to Society/ World*
Purpose	Mission + Fiduciary	Mission + Fiduciary + Operations	Mission + Fiduciary + Operations + Strategy	Mission + Fiduciary + Operations + Strategy + Contribution to Society/World
Deliberations	Consent Agenda and Private Conversations	Consent Agenda + Discussion and Debate in the boardroom	Consent Agenda + Discussion and Debate + Purposeful Dialogue	Consent Agenda + Discussion and Debate + Purposeful Dialogue + Discernment
Structures	Authority Centered	Shared Responsibility	Adaptive	Unifying
Relationships	Social Network	Group Membership	Trusting Partnership	Commitment to Community
Membership	Individual	Colleague	Partner	Global Citizen

Tool #1:
See Tasks as a Change Lever

We start with *tasks* in this overview because they are the most visible indicators of where on the continuum a board truly resides. Board tasks point to board values and the focus of meetings. Tasks show up in the content of meetings and the bias of that content. Tasks shape the focus and boundaries of deliberations.

Expand the work of a board and you begin changing its purpose and its identity. A board has routinely reviewed the financial reports, including the annual budget, for accuracy and integrity. If they start asking senior management to show how the budget aligns with the strategic plan, they have redefined the work of both the board and a few of the officers. The board's relationship with senior management and officers shifts in authority and different conversations are stimulated about the future of the organization. A "simple request" initiates significant change.

How Tasks Function at the Four Stages of Conscious Governance

- *Consent* Board tasks support the CEO's priorities, approve the consent agenda as put forth by the chief executive and board chair and fulfill fiduciary responsibilities.

- *Working* Board expands its tasks to include understanding operations in order to fully engage the business model and oversee performance in the marketplace.

- *Strategic* Board tasks add a longer term horizon; board tasks at this level center on assuring sound vision, direction and navigation, and employing systems thinking and strategic thinking.

- *Mindful* Board tasks expand to include diligent inquiry into how the organization and its actions impact the external community, society and the planet.

Employing the tool of tasks means inserting new work into committee and plenary meetings while ensuring that the essential existing tasks continue.

Tool #2:
See Purpose as a Change Lever

A board's *purpose* (or purposes) is partially documented in the organization's by-laws, charters, and other legal documents. It also lives in the board's culture. Purpose always connects to fulfilling the organization's mission/vision, sponsoring talented leadership, and assuring financial integrity.

How Purpose Functions at the Four Stages of Conscious Governance

At every stage, board *purpose* includes fiduciary oversight and protecting the organization's tangible and intangible assets as defined by the history and values of the enterprise.

- A *Consent* Board focuses on fulfilling the mission of the organization and fiduciary responsibilities, defined legally and bound by institutional culture. Most boards include hiring and wholeheartedly supporting the chief executive until performance of the executive or organization falls. The board exercises it authority to fire the CEO. The context for the Consent Board is the CEO's ability to lead the organization's performance ethically. The timeframe is the current year.

- *Working* Board's purpose carries forward all the Consent Board's responsibilities and adds understanding of operational and product performance. The context is the organization, its markets, and competitors. The timeframe is 1-3 years.

- *Strategic* Board purpose carries forward fiduciary oversight and operational knowledge. It adds the understanding of the strategy for long-term success and sustainability of the enterprise beyond the typical horizon. The context expands to include regions, economies, and resources. The timeframe stretches to 10 years or more.

- *Mindful* Board brings forward everything in the first three stages as purpose expands to overseeing the impact of the enterprise on community, society and the world. The context is a meaningful contribution to humankind. The timeframe is in perpetuity.

Employing the tool of purpose means expanding the board's identity and their shared belief in why the board exists in the first place. Many generative conversations between individuals and among the group are required. Expanded purpose is a sign the transformation is underway.

Tool # 3:
See Deliberations as a Change Lever

Deliberations include discussion, debate, dialogue, and decision-making. These activities embody the board's collective thinking *in action*. *The quality of deliberations* determines the breadth and depth of engagement with issues regardless of the board's decision-making structure (voting versus consensus) and foreshadows the robustness of decisions.

How Deliberations Function at the Four Stages of Conscious Governance

Board member expectations of appropriate deliberations can be dramatically different. They will need to adjust how they speak up, listen to each other, disagree and agree, pose questions, name patterns apparent in the board's deliberations, and willingly "name the elephant in the room."

- *Consent* Board deliberations are controlled by the board chair and CEO. Deliberations are bounded by the consent agenda and tightly managed. Disagreement is usually aired outside the boardroom. Consent Board deliberations are viewed as efficient and contained.

- *Working* Board deliberations are more inclusive with a strong reliance on committees as the venue for conversation and debate prior to plenary discussions. They are less bounded and less predictable in terms of the outcome. Plenary session discussions are longer and may be separated from the consent agenda vote.

- *Strategic* Board deliberations are infused with "out of the box" conversations in which issues are framed in the future and outside experts are invited in to shake up the board's thinking. They believe in exploring ideas that combine creativity and disciplined analysis. Deliberations focus on integrating data and results and occur within more flexible meeting structures. There is more emphasis on deliberations of the whole rather than the parts (committees). Spotting trends and patterns is everyone's responsibility.

- *Mindful* Board deliberations move from the external world inward and then back outward as the board considers the impact of decisions and actions from a much longer term and purposeful perspective. Social, political and economic experts may be invited guests the evening before a meeting as Mindful Board members prepare for the next day's deliberations.

To employ the tool of deliberations you will need to allocate enough time in the meeting agenda and carefully craft the questions that will open up a generative dialogue. Be prepared for reluctance to participate fully, strong differences of opinion, more questions, and important insights.

Tool #4:
See Structures as a Change Lever

A systems principle applies here: structure determines performance. **Structures** that drive board behavior include the policies, practices, and traditions of the board. They are both visible and opaque, and are always present in how a board operates. Meeting schedules and standard agendas, leadership roles and expectations, expression of power and authority, composition of

> Using structures as a change lever may be the most difficult because it requires changing people's minds about the most visible traditions and altering carefully constructed processes and boundaries.

committees, by-laws, the decision-making model, membership rules, and group behavior norms are all examples of vital and determinative structures.

Structures come from a board's mental models of what is good and right governance based on their experience and beliefs. Leadership is a vital structure in Conscious Governance. It is a visible and invisible force; it influences how formal leadership roles are defined and enacted, it influences how the board and CEO relate, and shapes the board-board chair relationship. Using structures as a change lever may be the most difficult because it requires changing people's minds about the most visible traditions and altering carefully constructed processes and boundaries.

How Structures Function at the Four Stages of Conscious Governance

- Structures in the *Consent* Board are highly bounded with clear rules and predictable processes, and are managed through the CEO-Board Chair leadership. Information is controlled. This board's structures are designed to provide assurance and containment.

- *Working* Board structures are more open, varied, and complex, providing a broader database. Committees are the work unit that brings recommendations forward for a vote. Structures support the board's knowledge and guidance of business and operational performance.

- *Strategic* Board structures intentionally facilitate strategic thinking and decision-making in full board conversations and across the committee boundaries. Information may come from inside or outside experts. Committees are usually less fixed and more adaptable to the strategic priorities.

- Structures in the *Mindful* Board support long-term considerations, inclusivity, and social responsibility. Information flows freely. Structures align with the needs of the organization and are grounded in the fiduciary and strategic obligations. The aim of Mindful Board structures is fulfilling the organization's purpose and capturing its potential.

Engaging structures as a tool means to design practices, procedures and paradigms to fit the new purpose of the board which will assess agendas, committees, and use of technology, for example, for "fit" with the new stage of governance.

Pay special attention to the necessary changes in the governance boundary—a formidable structure—between the board and officers along the continuum. The boundary changes from a fortified wall with one formal opening in the Consent Board to a fluid permeable boundary in the Mindful Board. People on both sides of the boundary can be confused and frustrated before learning how to relate to the other group.

Tool # 5:
See Relationships as a Change Lever

The quality of relationships between board members, among the board and CEO and senior officers, and between the board and constituents is the "magic sauce" in board performance. Good, healthy relationships foster good governance. Unhealthy or damaged relationships have wide-reaching consequences for the organization; take note of the well-publicized dysfunction of the Hewlett-Packard board in the early 2000s. Relationships are the "container," strong or flimsy, that holds deliberations. As one governance guru told us, "Chemistry is the first thing and everything in an effective board."

How Relationships Function in the Four Different Stages of Conscious Governance

- *Consent* boards tend to have strong social connections with the chief executive. New members tend to come from board members' existing social or work networks. People tend to be congenial and follow the chief executive's lead. Receiving only technical reports proscribes relationships between other officers and board members.

- A *Working* Board does its work through committees where the relationships and deliberations are strongest. Members, selected for their talents and skills, respect other committees' recommendations and value their leadership in related deliberations. Senior officers enter into a working relationship with the board as liaisons to board committees. Board and officers can develop a strong working partnership.

- *Strategic* Boards have more diversity in perspectives and capabilities. Tasks have expanded from fiduciary and operational to include strategic; each of those perspectives needs representation. The board must be clear with officers about the board's role as thinking partners and who "owns" strategy creation. The relationship between the board and officers, especially the CEO, is more inclusive and interdependent without confusing the legal boundaries between the board and management.

- *Mindful* Board members share a higher order of responsibility beyond the walls of the organization. Their relationships represent the reach of the enterprise and may be frustrating at times for the traditional board member. They consult outside experts for input into deliberations. Officers must understand a Mindful Board's expanded work to avoid their discounting the board's value to the organization and its future.

Engaging relationships as a tool requires emotional intelligence, experience with group dynamics, and the ability to build a sense of belonging among the members and officers. It means getting the most out of the people who are there to govern.

Tool #6:
See Membership as a Change Lever

Membership is the central nervous system of the board. Too much similarity or diversity can cause a malfunction, so it's important to get the right balance of people for the work of the board. *Three dimensions of membership matter* in Conscious Governance: 1) the explicit and implicit criteria and process for selecting new members; 2) evaluation of performance, individually and collectively; and 3) an opportunity for an individual to bring her/his heart, mind and voice in the boardroom.

How Membership Functions at the Four Different Stages of Conscious Governance

- *Consent* Board members are recruited to be supporters of the CEO and his/her agendas. They should be "good team players who know how to get in line and keep the game moving," but not at the cost of their integrity or reputation of the board. People with obvious conflicting viewpoints are identified and carefully vetted before an invitation to join is issued.

- *Working* Board members are recruited for their individual expertise and experience—especially for committee assignments. Skills and Talent Grids are often used to identify gaps in the board's capabilities. An individual can make a meaningful contribution to the success of the board and the institution by filling a gap in the board's required capabilities.

- Individuals are recruited to the *Strategic* Board for their ability to see, interpret and anticipate strategic issues over a significant time. They should be able to collaborate with other board members as well as officers to test and refine the strategic direction when needed. Ongoing fiduciary duties and operational knowledge require that some board members maintain the practical focus for the board. Diversity becomes a benefit and a curse.

- People recruited for the *Mindful* Board can use their insights to help the board anticipate and interpret patterns and trends from multiple sources and industries. They tend to be passionate advocates who can facilitate or block deliberations. Boards need the perspective of systems thinkers such as social and political scientists and environmentalists. These are examples of the diverse people needed to understand the impact of the organization on stakeholders, society, and the planet.

Employing membership as a tool means recruiting the right people to join the evolving board and asking some people to leave. This tool requires diplomacy, compassion, and courage.

Get Ready for One More Powerful Ingredient

In the next chapter we examine becoming the mindful board member.

How to Talk About These Ideas

The goal of this chapter is to introduce you to the six tools for leading the journey along the Continuum of Conscious Governance. Hopefully you see how each tool impacts board work and culture in each of the four stages. Here are talking points for your use.

If we want to change our board, what do we need to do?

"There is a set of tools we can use to get our board moving to the next stage without having to go shopping for them. These tools are elements that already exist on any team: *tasks, purpose, deliberations, structures, relationships, and membership.* We've worked with them at past team retreats but in a different way. We can use these same tools to change our board. The key is to use all of them as an integrated set."

How do we know which ones to use when?

"Each board is different, so you have to start where your board is. Keep in mind, using these tools one at a time will only get us incremental change. To make it all the way to the next stage, we will have to plan how to use all six tools in different combinations."

How do we use these things as tools?

"Tasks—call them responsibilities—can be broadened and the board has to learn how to think and work differently to incorporate the new work. They're moving on their way down the path!

Changing a board's purpose is serious business. You've just told the board their basic charter or identity has changed. Board members have to really understand their mission, the context and timeframe.

Using deliberations as a tool often means opening up the debates and dialogues to everyone on the board in plenary sessions. Those chats in the parking lots and private phone calls aren't the only way to handle different opinions. We need to value both disagreement and consensus.

Structures can be tricky. We can change committees around, expand agendas, add new reports, and even routinely invite outsiders to our board meetings. Those changes in old ways of doing things could stir up some people. It's when we have to change people's minds about tightly-held beliefs that it gets difficult. Moving from Consent Board to a Working Board is probably the biggest renovation of the board's mindset and structure. Our board will need persistence and patience.

Changing relationships is interesting work. As you move along the continuum, potential relationships open up beyond friends of the CEO or board. The board changes from a network of friends to a working team to a planning group. Diversity and expertise become more important along the way. We have to have good facilitation skills and emotional intelligence to use this tool.

Membership is a firecracker. Start changing the members of a board and watch some sparks fly. People may be asked to leave because they don't want to change to fit the new board. Other people will be recruited to join the board for what they can contribute in expertise and time.

I can see how each tool can make a difference. Imagine the impact when we get all six tools working. That should crank up the momentum to transform!"

What's the connection between the tools and the disciplines?

"The disciplines are the practices we need to develop continuously so we can master Conscious Governance. The endpoint on the Continuum of Conscious Governance is the Mindful Board. These six tools will help our board move along the continuum and continue to grow in our understanding and practice of the disciplines.

For example, *developing leadership by the group will require respectful relationships* and Members who are willing to share leadership across the board. The board can't be a collection of community celebrities! Everyone also needs to understand how only shared leadership can facilitate the purpose of the board, as in Strategic and Mindful boards.

Another example is the *role of deliberations and relationships in the practice of fearless engagement.* Individuals have to believe it's safe to challenge and trust that others will respect it.

The disciplines and tools together comprise a dynamic model of Conscious Governance."

Prescient's Journey—
Starting the Transition to Working Board

The transformation from Consent Board to Working Board is the most difficult of the three transitions because it requires a radical shift in perspective and practice. Prescient's board has been on a steep learning curve, fueled by recognizing how important the board's transformation is to Prescient's future. As you will see in Part 2, the

> **The transformation from Consent Board to Working Board is the most difficult of the three transitions because it requires a radical shift in perspective and practice.**

process of transformation from one stage to the next requires using all the tools. In this installment of the story, all six elements become critical tools for making the transition.

The ad hoc strategic planning group dives in

As promised, Marc follows up from the retreat and appoints a four-member ad hoc strategic planning committee: Bob, Suzanne, Charles and George. The four of them bring a strong background of for-profit and non-profit management, financial management, executive leadership, entrepreneurship and community relations. Marc feels this group brings the best balance of energies and perspectives. He also thinks a small group would be best to contain the work and get it finished.

Marc charges the ad hoc committee to review data about the current external environment, Prescient's current state, and any information about trends. With this material as background, the committee is to collaborate with Jim to draft a set of five-year strategic imperatives or goals and bring their recommendation to the board at the next meeting. Marc makes it clear he expects the group to work closely with Jim, and include Kim and Zach in their discussions as needed. Suzanne asks Marc who will lead the ad hoc committee. "George," says Marc, without missing a beat.

The board's standing committees have generally operated within tightly defined charters. This is the first time an ad hoc committee is used to address a strategy/operations issue. As the ad hoc group gets to work, George gives his fellow work group members several articles on strategy as well as a book he found recently on how governing boards need to lead actively when necessary. It takes some time for Jim and his senior team to feel comfortable and not criticized by this bold move. In fact, once the work gets underway, he confesses to George he feels more supported by the board than ever before.

The result is that, in addition to focusing on the strategic planning work, the ad hoc committee becomes a think tank of sorts about the board. This is not without its challenges. Suzanne, in particular, constantly expresses worry that such conversations are "out of bounds." Jim is not worried. He finds himself stepping back and seeing the value of the energy and ideas the group is generating.

The ad hoc committee dives into its work with startling energy. As they work with Jim, Kim, and Zach, the board members find themselves asking more questions and learning more about the enterprise. Over the next two board meetings, the committee brings more information and more questions for the board's consideration.

While board members find the dialogue energizing, officers start to get cranky and sensitive to the board's "intrusion" into their sphere of influence. The "glow" of the ad hoc committee conversations fades when the whole board starts to ask tough questions. After the second meeting, Jim approaches Marc in a state of frustration and anger. "What is happening with the board? Do they want to run the business?!"

Notice the use of the tools

Forming the ad hoc strategic planning committee is turning out to be a powerful experience for this board and CEO. The very creation of such a group has started to bring to the foreground the differences among board members in their individual philosophies and beliefs about strategy and operations. The use of structure as a tool is generating new questions and broadening the board's view of the situation. It is also opening up key questions about committee roles, information flow and committee performance (structures, tasks, relationships, purpose, and deliberations).

Suzanne's reluctance and concerns are very typical of traditional board members. In her attempts to slow things down or raise cautionary questions, she has actually helped the ad hoc group—and ultimately the whole board—to look at what they are doing with greater consciousness and self-awareness.

Then a defining moment occurs

Marc calls George to meet for lunch. After a few minutes of conversation, Marc takes a deep breath and charges forward. He shares his concern about the board and all the "annoying questions" members are asking. He is worried the board is too involved and on a path that might just lead to the CEO's resignation and unfavorable press. "George, I trust your take on the situation and this board. What should I do? What can I do to support Jim and keep this board on track?"

"Marc, my organization's been through a strategic planning process and the questions being asked by our board members are good ones. It makes sense to get input from several constituent groups—as the committee is pressing Jim and Zach to do. First, let the strategic planning group do its work and bring back to the board, with Jim, their findings and recommendations. And, Marc, I've been thinking a lot about how our board's doing and how we could be governing differently."

With one eyebrow raised, Marc signals George to continue. George responds, "Isn't it time for us, all of us, to get more engaged? Isn't it time for us to really understand more about the business model and the strategy? This, as you know, is not the same thing as running the business."

"Say more, George."

George sits back and takes a deep breath. "First let's wait and see what the strategic planning group brings forward at the upcoming meeting. I think we've made good progress on the issues. It seems that board members have expectations of Jim we need to talk about so that he can feel confident we have his back. Beyond that, I think that if our committees and the board as a whole were more engaged, we could help Jim and his team more effectively. Right now, we listen and vote, but we are not having much needed conversations. We need to work together. We need to learn how to work together. Now may very well be the time to become that board."

Marc looks at George, nods, and is quiet for a quite a long time.

Several months pass

The ad hoc strategic planning group gives its report to the board. Led by Bob, the group presents a set of recommendations. Jim offers his endorsement of the ideas, but makes it clear he wants to know what the full board thinks of the new strategic imperatives. Marc reminds the group he expects Jim and his officers to take any recommendations from the board and revise the strategic plan.

The presentation includes more questions about the external environment, operations and future options for strategic action, igniting intense discussion. Nearly every board member speaks up to ask a question, offer a comment or opinion, to endorse a point of view, or to disagree. The meeting is later described as "very loud."

After a lengthy conversation, it becomes clear the board, as a whole, does not want to disband the ad hoc strategic planning committee. However, some express doubts as Marc and George start to respond to this unusual request. Suzanne, in particular, criticizes the board's eagerness to pursue the strategic planning related tasks. "Isn't that why we have Jim as CEO?" Her comment grabs Marc's attention and the memory of lunch with George flashes through his brain.

A special executive committee meeting is called

After that very loud board meeting, Jim approaches Marc. While Jim states his appreciation for the new ideas the ad hoc committee generated, Marc recognizes Jim's anxiety about the board's confidence in his leadership. He promises Jim he will speak to the executive committee and get Jim some feedback. Marc quickly convenes a special executive committee meeting to test the board's confidence in the CEO.

The executive committee meeting is reassuring and unsettling for Marc. The committee members all express confidence in Jim—for now. The discussions about the strategy and future of the organization have struck a chord with each person. Bob, who also chairs the audit committee, asks, "We all seem to be fine with Jim's leadership. He and the officers are trying to give us the data we request. But when will we know we have enough data? We can't just keep depending on management for all the answers. We have to have our own point of view of the situation—grounded in real information and realistic assumptions."

As happened at the board meeting, this leads to a vigorous—though somewhat tangential—conversation about the board's committees, what the board has been talking about in meetings, and how to navigate the need for more information without alienating Jim or anyone else, for that matter.

Marc watches and listens. He realizes the conversation is more about the board members' genuine concern about the changing market, operational effectiveness and the board's ability to govern than it is about Jim as a CEO.

What has happened?

It was a critical moment when Marc realizes that the executive committee conversation was less about Jim than it was about strategy and how the board conducts its business. He is using the disciplines of reflection and self-awareness to monitor his own reactions and listen deeply to the group.

He is still confused about next steps, but it looks like he will be able to avoid a mistake that could damage Prescient. This insight points to the vital role of board chair as both facilitator and interpreter. When things get messy at the beginning of a transition, the board chair and other mindful board members play a key role in keeping the momentum going and on track.

The tools will help lead the board to becoming a Working Board. For example, the structure of the ad hoc committee made it safe for deliberations to take on new questions and topics. Notice that the board is now questioning the committee structure—evidence of how the success of the ad hoc group made it possible to consider additional changes. Members are using the disciplines of expanded consciousness and fearless engagement while respecting the trust everyone—including Jim and the officers—must have for the individuals and the process. Marc's decision to appoint those four people speaks to his understanding of the board's membership and individual talents. George, as a mindful board member, is both an informal leader and a role model for the group—two attributes the board and officers need right now.

The Prescient board still needs to come to terms with the change in tasks and purpose, but the windows are opening.

Chapter 5

Become the Mindful Board Member

You might well ask: Then how are we to practice mindfulness? My answer is: keep your attention on the work, be alert and ready to handle ably and intelligently any situation which may arise—this is mindfulness. Mindfulness is the miracle by which we master and restore ourselves.

— Thich Nhat Hanh, *The Miracle of Mindfulness*

No matter where you sit in the boardroom—literally or figuratively—you can make a difference in how the board performs and transforms. Your power as a mindful board member comes from your showing up and contributing to the board's practice of governance, balancing your independent voice with your belonging to the group.

Until now, this book has focused primarily on the full board—a human system charged with fulfilling a significant role for an enterprise and society. The *disciplines and tools* of Conscious Governance have emphasized the transition and transformation of the group.

> **An attuned board member can make the difference between a board that runs on automatic or practices vibrant discernment.**

Conscious Governance begins with the individual board member who makes a commitment to serve an organization. The mindful board member adds commitment to the board's effectiveness and to her/his meaningful use of precious personal time.

Have You Ever Played Jazz?

Playing jazz is a good metaphor for being a mindful board member. Jazz is a journey of simultaneous individual and group endeavor. Each musician feels and hears the past, present and future directions of the group's creativity and either joins or embellishes the musical flow with notes or silence or keen awareness. She or he has the power to lift the ensemble to another level of play and surpass their expectations. They all become more conscious of what is possible.

Miles Davis could do that time and again. He said, "Don't just play what's there. Play what's not there." The essential mindful board member is attuned to not only what is being said, but what is left unspoken in the "jazz combo" that is the board where you serve. A mindful trustee or director can sense and make sense of the undercurrents—positive and negative—that flow through conversation and deliberations. Being "in-between" ideas that are predictable and those that are emergent includes paying attention to the less tangible aspects of board reality while staying alert to what is going on in the room. Sensing the group's past, present and future direction is as vitally important to Conscious Governance as completing tasks and casting votes. An attuned board member can make the difference between a board that runs on automatic or practices vibrant discernment.

The power of a mindful board member is an energy and spirit that enliven her work of governance but also the relationships and work of the board. He is more aware of how to make a valuable contribution and how the mission of the organization connects to his personal purpose. Board work becomes meaningful, not just convenient or opportunistic, as an important way to play what's in her or his mind and learn new jazz combinations by creating with others.

Start at the Beginning

Three disciplines begin with individual practice: self-awareness, reflection, and trustworthiness. Disciplines demand life-long study and practice. Start with the discipline that interests you the most.

Practice Self-Awareness

In Conscious Governance, *self-awareness* helps you decide which boards and committee assignments align with your talents, capabilities and preferences. The outer practice of self-awareness means truly knowing who you are—"I know what I believe, what I can do and what I want to do in the world"—and testing yourself in real circumstances. The inner practice means being able to center yourself and become aware of your inner thoughts and feelings. You are curious to uncover any dimensions and capabilities that constitute your "self" well beyond what might be immediately apparent to yourself or others.

Self-awareness is also your ability to monitor your reactions in the moment and then see how your interactions and style affect others. It is as if you can see yourself from the balcony perspective as you enter the boardroom and engage with others and the tasks at hand. A mindful board member opens to the possibility of deeper understanding of self and embraces personal change through being in relationship with others and being engaged in the tasks of the group.

The Greek word *gnosis*—seeing and knowing beyond what is obvious—arises from openness to new possibilities about ourselves and the world that engages us. We are to use our awareness to contemplate the many influences beyond the institution.

In the context of the current board you serve, what is your self-identity? Who are you becoming? Write down your social roles, values, and goals. Consider how your identity fits within the board culture and where you know there are differences. Do your differences augment or diminish the board's effectiveness? For example, you may be the person who can lighten up any serious conversation with humor, but a couple of times you've gotten "that look" from a few board members admonishing you. Or you are masterful at summarizing a messy conversation and the board has recognized your contribution.

How do you want to grow and develop in your term on the board? You can have goals to build your personal capabilities—leading small groups, setting strategic direction, understanding global marketing, as examples. If you want to broaden your professional network, how will you get to know other members? If board work is your encore career, what difference do you want to make for yourself and the organization?

In discovering who we are and why, we master and restore ourselves.

Trustworthy Relationships

All work is done through relationships. The quality of work depends on the quality of relationships. *Trustworthy relationships are vital* to any work group.

Relationships have two sides—self and other. Start with your model of trustworthiness. What do you believe you must do to be seen as trustworthy? In a study we conducted several years ago, interviewees identified 21 characteristics of "trustworthiness." For example, as a trustworthy person you

- do what you say you will do,

- tell the truth as you know it,

- don't hurt others intentionally,

- admit mistakes,

- make it safe to talk about dreams and concerns,

- and, are willing and able to do the work assigned to you. (See the Appendix for the Work Team Trust Survey)

Recall feedback you've received. Are you seen as trustworthy?

Imagine a basket of trust for you to give to someone else, indicating he/she is trustworthy. When you begin working with someone new, do you slide the basket over to the person saying, "I trust you until you prove me wrong?" Or, do you hold onto the basket for some time until the other person has "proven" trustworthiness? As you build trustworthy relationships with other board members, remember they may have a different idea about giving trust.

People are more likely to follow someone they believe understands them. A mindful board member is conscious of others' understanding of governance and their feelings about changing the basic identity of the board. The practice requires knowing board colleagues, paying attention to what is happening in the room at a given point in time, and recognizing how internal and external realities are influencing board deliberations.

Along the path of Conscious Governance, the full board needs to attend to their relationships. You can help. Pay attention to the boundary between the board and officers who comprise the full governance community for the organization. Are their relationships trustworthy? The combined group of board and officers is a dynamic human system that requires even more skillful attuning to others. Interactions—whether as social exchanges or serious deliberations—illustrate the formal and informal power and authority in a group. During plenary sessions and committee meetings, "read the room" by noticing and following both what is said and what is not being said. Listen deeply to the messages, ideas, intentions and feelings below the surface of the spoken words.

Proactively exercise your strong relationship skills to catalyze and lead from one stage of Conscious Governance to the next. Employ your ombudsman skills to keep board members in healthy relationships. Show how to value and take advantage of the circle of people with diverse backgrounds, paradigms and talents who come together to serve the organization. No board member can be left behind if each one is coming along at his/her own speed. A mindful board member is attuned to the talents and tolerances of each member and has an idea how to bring those talents into alignment for fulfilling fiduciary tasks, deliberating critical issues, and achieving a new level of performance.

Reflection

Reflection is looking in a mirror to see what is not visible any other way. Practicing reflection allows you to see what is behind and supporting your opinions and actions and how they fit (or not) into the prevailing mental models of your board. What do you think the organization's mission requires the board to do? Are the officers aligned with your model of leadership? Do you believe board members interact in ways to get their work done effectively? After your first answer to these questions, ask yourself, "Why do I believe that?" You begin to see what has been hidden behind your thinking. You have an opportunity to change your mind. A mindful board member needs to be facile in personal reflection to understand the opinions and models he holds as good and right. As she gains skill, she can demonstrate for others what is involved.

Difference, uncertainty, emotional content, and opposition are a few triggers for reflection. Reflection isn't easy even when we can quiet ourselves. We may be able to retrieve the thoughts at hand, but we also have tacit knowledge tucked away. It takes skillful inquiry to access our thinking behind our polished thoughts. Will we have to change our minds? Is the discussion challenging one of our fundamental beliefs? How do we feel about that?

Time and quiet allow you to sequester yourself to find out what you believe is reality, how you value elements of reality, what opinions you hold, and what solutions you would consider. Reflection is essential to learning. Until we know what we believe we cannot enhance our own thinking. Reflection is even more difficult when we have to reflect while listening to an expert presentation or engaging in a sensitive conversation. Mastery is learning how to reflect while in the action, in real-time.

In a group, the mindful board member is lead scout, taking the group into their thinking and noticing where there are similarities and differences, undiscussables, and irrelevant beliefs, as examples. Board members have diverse points of view and opinions that aren't always expressed but become drivers of hidden agendas. The mindful board member is willing and able to lead the group into their collective thinking and shared models.

The basic tool you can use is powerful questions that force others to reflect and open their minds to new possibilities. Examples are: What more is behind your question? What leads to you say that? How does that fit with the way you see it?

Group reflection creates vulnerability that can be a barrier to overcome. Participating in reflection requires that we make our thinking explicit in a public setting where our thoughts can be challenged. The individual becomes vulnerable as her/his thinking is challenged. The mindful board member makes it safe by demanding respect and focus on the ideas, and summarizing frequently. A second barrier is the lack of communication skills of inquiry, suspending disbelief, and dialogue. Some people turn reflection into a debate, but a heated debate with defended positions is a sign the process is not working. Group reflection gets messy and can become frustrating with so many questions and possible answers in the room. In the context of the boardroom, members may perceive the loss of control or a bad process. The mindful board member is able to be a calm presence and gently guide the group into testing its current thinking and processes against changing contexts.

Conscious Governance asks the board to know where they are on the Continuum and what evidence supports their assessment. Each stage challenges board members to change their minds about effective governance. Buy-in can't happen until each individual member reflects on what he/she thinks is working and not working about current governance practices. Then members can consider what they gain by moving to the next stage. As the board transitions, they must be able to reflect-in-action—talk about their experience of what is working and not working well for them to fulfill their governance responsibilities.

Reflection promotes discovery and advances transformation.

As you practice the first three disciplines, you will learn whether you and the current board members are aligned. Others have likely noticed ways you approach your trusteeship. Some may have joined you in leading the group toward more self-awareness, reflection, and trustworthy relationships.

Create a Cohort for the Collective Disciplines

The mindful board member knows he can't transform the board by himself. He will need to find others who believe the board needs to transform. This group of *people who are willing to lead the transformation can begin the study and practice of the three collective disciplines: expanded conscious, fearless engagement, and leadership by the group.*

> **A board moving along the Continuum is always expanding its knowledge and awareness to adapt to new governance demands.**

Mindful board members have work to do. They demonstrate what each discipline looks like in action. As the board makes progress, the cohort of mindful board members can enroll others to learn about the disciplines and coach the board in its practice of all the disciplines.

Expanded Consciousness

A board moving along the Continuum is always expanding its knowledge and awareness (both elements of consciousness) to adapt to new governance demands. Mindful board members realize they have chosen to raise their standard of performance and broaden their scope of influence. The organization's contexts are changing. The goal of this discipline is to seek more information and knowledge about the organization and its impact. The board is committed to learning.

A Working Board begins to recruit members with specific subject matter or technical expertise needed on the board. This new board member with an innovative or atypical idea may struggle to be heard at the board meeting. Where in the agenda does the new idea fit? A mindful board member can redirect this expert member's contribution to committee meetings, committee reports in plenary session, and board retreats. Agendas can accommodate learning sessions for the full board when appropriate.

To expand the consciousness of the board, mindful board members may distribute articles or books to set up an important conversation. Speakers from inside in industry or futurists focusing on global markets are another way to stretch a board's consciousness to include new ideas. Site visits are another method.

> **The board has to reach a level of mastery of the other disciplines before it will recognize and value fearless engagement.**

There are several ways for a board to continue to grow its knowledge and awareness. Identify what the board needs to learn to adapt to the organization's changing contexts. Set a learning agenda. *The cohort of mindful board members holds themselves accountable for the board's practice of expanded consciousness.*

Fearless Engagement

An individual exercises this discipline, but only with the support of the board and its culture. The board has to reach a level of mastery of the other disciplines before it will recognize and value fearless engagement. A passion for the truth as we can know it, the sustainability of the organization, and a commitment to the practice of governance drive the respectful challenge of the board's thinking and actions.

Mindful board members must be attuned to the board's readiness to be challenged. There are right and wrong times to wade into discussing board performance, dysfunctions, mistaken beliefs, or outdated governance models.

Fearless engagement allows a courageous board member to describe what she has learned or sees going on in the boardroom, C-suite, or marketplace. She recognizes her perception may be flawed so she engages with humility. Ground rules set by the board are an important structure to support fearless engagement by those speaking and those listening. Respect for the individual, board, and institution is paramount.

Along the Continuum, board diversity increases. Diversity can hinder or support fearless engagement. The mindful cohort develops its skills in leading and facilitating challenging conversations. They know how to create a safe environment for people to agree and disagree and they remain attuned to all members as the conversations progress. They also make clear the purpose of the challenge: to consider a new idea, to change the work process of the board, to make a decision, for example.

A Strategic Board and Mindful Board cannot excel without the practice of fearless engagement. While in the Working Board stage, intentionally begin developing this discipline.

Leadership by the Group

Mindful board members recognize the unique contribution each board member can make to governance. Allocating leadership to one or two positions doesn't make sense when the consciousness of the board is expanding beyond the walls of the organization and diverse members have been recruited for their talents and skills to lead in new contexts. The board is rich with capabilities. *When leadership by the group is fully realized, expect everyone to participate.*

Assume that a diverse group can learn to manage itself with a few accepted structures in place. *Leadership by the group* strives to optimize the knowledge, experience, and commitment of a talented board. Mindful board members ask for reactions, experience, and data from board members who can shine a light on the board's deliberations.

Leadership by the group does not abandon formal leadership roles. The board chair is keeper of the vision and mission while encouraging and guiding deliberations. From the position of board chair, this person senses when to call for a vote and when to suggest more time before deciding. Committee chairs manage the attention of the board on their committee's work. The difference in carrying out their roles is the distribution of power and authority.

As the scope of board work expands, mindful board members step in to lead and enroll others to lead with their expertise and commitment. They may be in a leadership role for one meeting, the span of an ad hoc committee, or two years as a committee chair.

Leadership by the group is dependent on the other five disciplines. This powerful discipline is the culmination of mindfulness through which "we master and restore ourselves" as individuals and a board and energize the organization in perpetuity.

You Have a Choice

Becoming a mindful board member asks you to study and practice the six disciplines. Developing your practice of these disciplines will serve you well in many settings.

> **Exercise your power by bringing your full self—your talents and skills, your insights and observations, and your spirit—into the boardroom.**

Exercise your power by bringing your full self—your talents and skills, your insights and observations, and your spirit—into the boardroom. Respect the concomitant responsibilities of humility and self-awareness. Shed light on what is unseen or unnoticed. Use powerful questions, your understanding of relationships among members, and your ability to guide others into alignment about the desired future. Have enough self-doubt to temper your managing and avoid dictating. Help others distinguish between change for the sake of improvement and the evolutionary change of transformation. Point out that transformation is messy and emergent and depends on trust and faith in others and yourself.

Are you ready to start your own journey of Conscious Governance?

Prescient's Mindful Board Members— Learning from Each Other

The individuals involved in Prescient's board are challenged by the situation and the opportunity to transform. Early on, George brings into the boardroom his ability to be a mindful board member, a gift and talent others benefit from over time. Developing and practicing the individual disciplines and then the group disciplines is a process of learning how to play jazz together as the board faces significant business issues together. Here are a few reflections from a couple of key players in the story.

One and half years after the first retreat

Jim looks out the window of his office. He has just ended a call with Marc, having reviewed the final draft of the upcoming board meeting agenda. He and the board have transformed. In the months leading up to the first retreat, he felt beleaguered and frustrated. Never before in his career had he been so openly challenged by the board. It felt bruising and unappreciative. He had even considered leaving, but wouldn't let them win—at least that's how he thought about the situation at the time. Oh, he wanted the board to be smarter, more strategy-savvy and less detached. He wanted their backs and their ability to help Prescient succeed. What he hadn't understood was that the board had to learn how to lead together and to engage differently to get where he wanted them to be.

He shakes his head. It still doesn't make a lot of sense at one level, but he has seen the results first hand. Who would have guessed? The hardest part was facing his personal limitations. Jim's ah-ha moment came eight months ago when he realized that he didn't have to go it alone and that he could ask board members to help. It was the scariest moment of his life. How could he the trust people who control his career? Yet they did help him without question.

He realizes that he has changed. He has become far more aware of how he jumps to conclusions and gets defensive without cause. George in particular has helped him see this part of himself, though comments from many of the other long-serving members also have pushed him to "get it." Laughing to himself, he considers how he now counts on the moments when someone says, "Can we take a moment and look at how we're thinking about this issue?"

ॐ

Sean leaves his office to have lunch with his best friend. The two of them have known each other since kindergarten. Sean maneuvers his beloved car into an impossibly small space in front of the restaurant. He wonders if the small space is a metaphor—sometimes the unlikely becomes reality. This singular insight becomes the topic of conversation over lunch. "Sarah, I know this is hard to believe," starts Sean, "But it's true. George and the others have really helped me over the past year, especially how my questions were pushing people away."

"Your questions, Sean?" asks Sarah. "You always ask the most amazing questions—you make people sit up and take notice!"

"I appreciate that, but I realized trying to be 'Socratic' and challenging the 'powers that be' doesn't always work in the boardroom. Actually it was something else that happened that made all the difference."

Sarah raises an eyebrow and leans across the table. "What? Tell me, Sean. I want to hear this."

"Well, believe it or not, I owe Suzanne a lot."

Sean sighs. "Here's what happened after a board meeting about six months ago."

Sean tells the story

At a board meeting rich with debate, and where everyone seemed to be contributing great insights about the next strategy wave, Sean noticed that Suzanne seemed to be unusually quiet. His experience of her was that she was the one first into the debate most of the time. He found himself unsettled by her new behavior. She didn't look distressed, angry or upset. She seemed watchful and paying attention to the conversation. "Weird," he thought.

Sean walked out of the meeting with Suzanne. Normally he prided himself on his "above the fray" persona, but this time something nudged at him and he turned to her. "Suzanne," he ventured, "What did you think of the meeting?"

She stopped in her tracks with a look of surprise on her face. "Sean, it was a great meeting. Why do you ask?"

Sean leaned in, "Because you were—different. I wondered what you were thinking."

Suzanne explained. "Sean, I got painful feedback from several people on this board that I was jumping in too quickly and not listening. I thought I was doing the right thing by defending Jim and Marc because they are the guys in charge. People didn't know if they could trust me." After a pause she continued. "When I started to slow down, I realized they were right. I had been missing the best parts of the conversation. I simply wasn't attuned to the group. It was as if I was running the meeting inside my own head. By paying more attention to my reactions before speaking, I find I can add value more easily because I'm not trying so hard. I'm hearing and seeing things so differently than before."

Sean looked at Suzanne in awe. He was about to say something when she continued, "There's one more thing. I didn't try to get to know everyone. I did not treat our colleagues with respect. I am changing that habit." Smiling, she turned and headed to her car.

George Notices

A little while later, as the board members are going to their cars, George watches Sean and Suzanne from a distance. He reflects on how Suzanne's commitment to becoming more mindful in her interactions with others has made it easier for more quiet members of the board to participate in deliberations. He noticed during the meeting that Sean kept looking at Suzanne, who was particularly quiet this time. He wonders about the conversation that is occurring. He hopes for the best.

See what we see: "We are in it together"

A lot has been going on during those months. Readiness to transform has been ripening. The general understanding of the external and internal contexts has increased steadily. The ad hoc group has become a critical mass of board members who can share insights and pull the board forward. The board is practicing all the disciplines—individually and collectively.

For these individuals the board's journey is also one of personal change and development. Jim, Sean and Suzanne all have had to develop the individual disciplines, which in turn influence the development of the group disciplines. Marc has demonstrated courage by not giving in to any one subgroup or to the discomfort expressed from time to time. He has stayed open to new possibilities. The benefit is a significant positive shift in trust and risk taking. By the close of this installment, George is no longer the only mindful board member!

One of the major shifts that occurred is the shift of "ownership of strategy" from exclusively the CEO and his team to a growing sense of partnership between management and the board. The ad hoc strategic planning group has served multiple purposes. Thanks to the skillful facilitation by George, the group has become a place to try out new ways of working together as well as completing the assigned task. When Prescient's board finally makes the full transition to Working Board, this early partnership experience serves them well as they continue to recalibrate how the system has performed.

While the board has yet to make lasting changes in each of the six elements, the way is opening up for transformational change.

PART 2: APPLY THE MODEL

Welcome to Part 2!

Here in Part 2 we describe *how* to apply the model and move your board from one stage of Conscious Governance to the next. We start with how to recognize when a board is ready to transform, followed by a careful look at each of the three major transitions.

- Chapter 6: Recognize **Readiness** to Transform

- Chapter 7: Recast the Limits: From **Consent Board to Working Board**

- Chapter 8: Expand the View from the Balcony: From **Working Board to Strategic Board**

- Chapter 9: Make Impact the Focus: From a **Strategic Board to Mindful Board**

Move from Readiness to Transformation

Here is a general framework to guide your action strategies all along the way. Each time you and your board decide to move from one stage to the next the emotional and intellectual challenges are distinct; the major steps are the same.

Did You Open the Book Here?

In this book, you can start anywhere, go anywhere. If you turned to this page to start, here are a few key ideas from Part 1 to help you navigate Part 2.

Know and Navigate the 4 Stages

There are four developmental stages a board moves through on the path of Conscious Governance: Consent Board, Working Board, Strategic Board and Mindful Board. As a board moves along the continuum, its members and the board as a whole expand their capabilities. The process is cumulative: each stage brings forward the capabilities from the previous stage(s) while developing new ones.

This is a developmental model, not a model for incremental change. What does that mean? It means a board's core purpose and "identity" transform. This is deep change; moving from one stage to the next is not tinkering at the edges. (Chapters 1 and 2)

The Continuum of Conscious Governance

Consent Board ➔ Working Board ➔ Strategic Board ➔ Mindful Board

The Boardroom—6 Tools

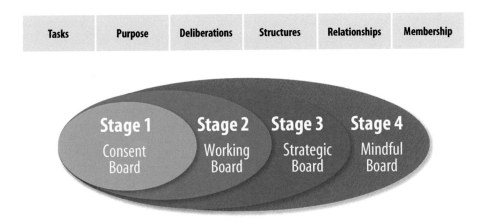

| Tasks | Purpose | Deliberations | Structures | Relationships | Membership |

Stage 1 Consent Board   **Stage 2** Working Board   **Stage 3** Strategic Board   **Stage 4** Mindful Board

Board Members and Officers—6 Disciplines

| Self-Awareness | Trustworthiness | Reflection | Expanded Consciousness | Fearless Engagement | Leadership by the Group |

The Path to the Mindful Board

Develop and Practice Six Disciplines

Conscious Governance is not possible without the practice of six vital disciplines: *self-awareness, trustworthiness, reflection, expanded consciousness, fearless engagement, and leadership by the group.* (Chapter 3) Disciplines are foundational. Without them, the changes are incremental, not developmental.

Ripen Readiness to Transform

We all know change—let alone transformation—doesn't happen unless there is adequate readiness to take on the job. Recognizing readiness (the R-Factor) involves heightened context intelligence, productive and provocative inquiry, and the presence of a committed core group ready to lead the process. (Chapter 6)

Employ Six Tools

We take the basic organization design elements present in every board and turn them into tools. They become change levers during the transition from one stage to the next, and sustain the momentum to fully transform. The tools are: *tasks, purpose, deliberations, structures, relationships and membership.* Read about how these elements as tools evolve as your board moves along the continuum in Chapter 4, "Open the Toolbox."

You use the tools to launch the transition—what we call "flip the switch" and "power up to transform"—to reach full transformation. (Chapters 7, 8 and 9)

Be a Mindful Board Member

All the way along the path you and your colleagues will make success possible as a mindful board member. (Chapter 5)

See how Prescient is doing

At the end of each chapter, we include an installment from *Prescient: A Tale of Transformation.* We illuminate the dynamics of Conscious Governance and becoming a Mindful Board through the story of Prescient, a fictional organization[5] we created based on our work and experiences with governing boards. The story begins with Chapter 1 and continues here in Part 2. The players are:

---

[5]Names, characters, the organization, events and incidents are either the products of the authors' imagination or used in a fictitious manner. Any resemblance to actual persons, living or dead, an actual organization, or actual events is purely coincidental.

Jim, the CEO of Prescient

Zach, vice president of marketing

Kim, CFO

Marc, board chair

George, mindful board member

Sean, "wild card" board member

Bob, Charles, Frank, Harry, John, Matt, Sam, Sophia, Suzanne, Todd, and Zoe are board members

Two new characters appear here in Part 2: Dave, Prescient's new Chief Operating Officer, and Eliza, a new board member.

Start the Journey

We begin now with the dramatic transition from Consent Board to Working Board. Buckle up!

Chapter 6

Invest in the R-Factor

A self changes when it changes its consciousness about itself. This is true for any system—individuals, organizations, societies. As the system develops a different awareness, this changed awareness will materialize as new responses. Thus, the source of change and growth for an organization or an individual is to develop increased awareness of who it is, now. If we take time to reflect together on who we are and who we could choose to become, we will be led into the territory where change originates.

— Meg Wheatley, *A Simpler Way*

Boards must navigate three major transitions successfully move along the Continuum of Conscious Governance from Consent Board to Mindful Board:

Consent Board to Working Board → **Working Board to Strategic Board** → **Strategic Board to Mindful Board**

Your most important move starts here with *readiness*. The transformational work associated with moving from one stage to the next calls for intense engagement of the heart and minds of individual board members and the entire group. Compare this level of commitment to the simple compliance needed for an incremental change. Most board members must be prepared to make a personal choice to expand their purpose and model of governance.

You must spend the right amount of time and effort assessing and helping the board become aware of its current relevance. If you assess the board's readiness and find there is enough willingness and capability to start the journey, you have increased your likelihood of success. If you ignore or rush through this assessment, you are likely to experience more struggle and possible failure.

Readiness is…

That point in time when the board is able to engage in the process of transformation, even if they are tentative. Readiness makes meaningful action possible. It pulls us forward with anticipation. It generates abundant energy available to tap.

Two early signs of readiness are dissatisfaction—often non-specific, and cause-seeking—trying to find the source of the dissatisfaction and fix it.

The pressure builds into three key indicators of readiness:

1. heightened context intelligence is evident in discussions at meetings;

2. productive and provocative inquiry raises consciousness of why the board is making certain decisions and what impact those decisions will have; and

3. a core group of board members are ready to lead the transformation effort.

You have readiness to transform—the R-Factor—when all three indicators are evident and occurring at the same time.

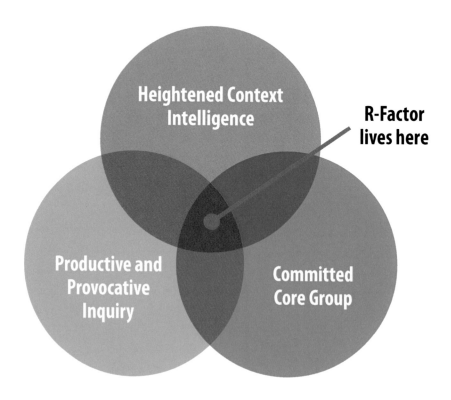

Most board development approaches do not require the R-Factor to implement because the strategies and techniques are incremental improvements, not transformational change. Moving along the Continuum of Conscious Governance is a transformational process that challenges purpose and identity. Attempts to transform in the absence of adequate readiness will not succeed. This is true for us as individuals and it is true in the boardroom.

Look for Early Signs of Readiness

Openness to change is usually preceded by dissatisfaction, often exhibited as unexpected disagreements. In the boardroom, these emotionally charged disagreements can break apart previous consensus and increase dissatisfaction with how the board or organization is performing. Very often the lack of specificity of these complaints—however small or large—makes it hard for board leadership to react. "I know something isn't right but I don't know exactly where to look." "We are being rushed into a decision when we need more time."

These eruptions seem to arise from much deeper concerns than those typically expressed in the course of deliberations. Expressed dissatisfaction increases intensity and sense of urgency in the board room. The board wants resolution and tends to look first outside of the boardroom for the cause of their discomfort. Is it the CEO, internal operations or management, customer demands, the industry, local economy, or new regulations? If they can isolate the cause, the board believes, it can implement a solution. Looking outward can be a function of fulfilling fiduciary responsibilities. However, when the eruptions are sudden, fuzzy or edgy, it's time to pay attention.

Readiness requires reflection at both the individual and group level. When board members look in the mirror at the board's effectiveness and see the gaps, they are ready to engage in transformation of the board. A board is not ready to transform if its focus remains on outside forces.

Every board—as a human system—has its own distinct personality, requiring you to engage in conversations with board leadership, informal leaders, and other concerned board members to assess what you are experiencing. Is there more going on than meets the eye?

Start with a Couple of Questions and See what Happens

When new disagreements occur, it's time to start asking questions. The most important questions to ask yourself and others at this point are:

- How is our dissatisfaction connected to the way we, the board, are governing?

- Is our dissatisfaction rooted more in the organization's performance?

- Are we analyzing the root-cause adequately? Are we jumping to conclusions?

- Are we truly prepared to answer the hard questions about who we are as a board and our willingness to transform how we govern?

Listen carefully to what is said and not said in response.

Ripen Emerging Readiness

Your assessment may show that you need to "ripen" the board's readiness over the next few months to build support for the journey. Ripening activities reframe the situation or issue to generate a strong sense of urgency. Three ways to ripen a situation are to start with an accepted issue and generalize from it, meet with small groups to build understanding, or have an authority figure propose immediate action. Do this with care to avoid damaging your credibility. Each transition depends on adequate readiness.

Confirm with a few trusted colleagues on the board that it is time to move forward. Reach agreement about your board's placement on the continuum. If you and others believe a critical mass of board members and senior officers are ready to begin the journey to the next stage on the continuum, you are ready to take action.

Remember, the Conscious Governance journey is developmental. As the board moves from one stage to the next, the board experiences deep and lasting changes in its purpose, skills, and focus. The board's internalized identity and culture transform. Every member will experience the journey differently. Leading the journey to a Mindful Board is both an art and a discipline. The "art" means adjusting the specific action steps to the unique characteristics of your enterprise and board. The "discipline" requires building and using the foundational disciplines with intention and persistence.

Look for the Indicators of Readiness

Recognize Heightened Context Intelligence

Heightened context intelligence is evidence of expanded consciousness. Board members and officers start discussing and questioning important internal and external pressures caused by events, trends, challenges, or opportunities. These pressures may signal that the business model, the industry and/or the economy are undergoing important shifts and changes. Beyond the ordinary oscillations that occur in any industry, these context pressures are the significant "bumps in the night" that wake board members and bring them to keen alertness. The evidence or indicators may also be just rising over the horizon, sending a weak alarm to their subconscious.

Context intelligence is more than awareness of a particular piece of the puzzle. Every enterprise and its board are nestled inside multiple contexts that shape the enterprise and the board's decision-making. These contexts are lenses through which we see what's happening inside and outside the enterprise. And, whether we are conscious of it or not, all four contexts we're about to describe are present in every deliberation and decision.

Move Gracefully Among the Four Contexts

Heighten your context intelligence by actively looking across the contexts, asking integrating questions, and introducing ideas and information from external sources into your deliberations. Rather than focusing on only one context, move gracefully among them—widening your collective view. At the most general level, there are four contexts we encounter all the time.

1. The first context is the **internal challenge or opportunity**—the budget, the product or service, the employees, the strategy, or the leadership, for example.

2. The second context sits on the boundary between the internal and external contexts. Sometimes we think of this as the contexts of **stakeholders or shareholders, constituents, or customers**. These are the groups of individuals, organizations, and services without which the enterprise would not exist.

3. The third context is **the industry or sector within which the organization resides** and which influences how operational and strategic issues are evaluated.

4. The fourth is **society and the social-political-economic-environmental forces** that press down on the sector, the marketplace and the enterprise.

These contexts make up the system of influence for any enterprise—non-profit or for-profit. Consciousness of that system and how we are governing within it influences both deliberations and actions taken as a result.

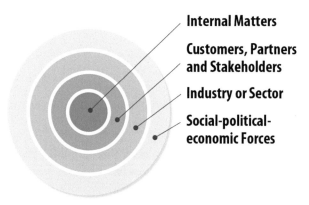

Internal Matters

Customers, Partners and Stakeholders

Industry or Sector

Social-political-economic Forces

Look for how the connections among the contexts are expressed in dialogue and in new questions that generate new discussions. When this occurs, context intelligence is expanding. As your board moves from one stage to the next, the nuances and complexity of each of these four major contexts become part of the board's context intelligence. The board and officers will become more attuned to the subsets within each of these four contexts and will use their insights when deliberating. When individuals and the group work together to learn what to anticipate and how to think about the contexts, the group is able to masterfully use context intelligence.

- Do you see signs that board members are proactively using the four contexts as a way to understand what lies ahead?

- Are board members expressing concern about the amount and type of information and data presented to the board in light of the context pressures?

- Is there a rising sense of disquiet about board deliberations and the board's grasp of the how the contexts are influencing your enterprise?

Practice Productive and Provocative Inquiry

Powerful questions, startling questions, and brand new questions are signs of readiness. Persistent, complicated queries are about our lives, individually and collectively, that defy clear solutions. Powerful questions direct us to something ambiguous and anxiety-producing in our reality. What are we most afraid of? What is our deepest hope for our customers? What wants to happen in our sector or community? Should we merge with a competitor to survive?

Something is in the air. Board members are fearlessly searching for insights. When one question leads to another, the interaction between heightened context intelligence and productive inquiry generates new energy and insights. People become connected to each other and their larger purpose at a deeper level of accountability.

From Public Files:

The board of Sweet Briar College in Virginia had to ask the existential question: Should we close the 114-year old College? They had tried to create a strategic plan in 2014 to remedy falling enrollments and financial pressures, but "the planning initiative did not yield any viable paths forward." Several small private schools were on the same edge. Chair of the board stated, "We have moral and legal obligations to our students and faculties and to our staff and to our alumnae. If we take up this decision too late, we won't be able to meet those obligations." The board's announcement to close Sweet Briar in August 2015 set off a passionate campaign by alumnae and friends to raise money for the College. Legal action to block the closing was taken that resulted in the full board's resignation and appointment of a new board as well as selection of a new president. The Washington Post on March 3, 2016 declared "the women's college has gone from doomed to resurrected but on life support, to something that is still fragile." The current board chair said, "Sometimes it takes a calamity to get people mobilized about something they care about."

One way to encourage productive inquiry is through outside speakers who expand consciousness and ripen readiness. They can ask provocative questions of the board and officers, questions that might otherwise be taboo or not yet considered.

As a mindful board member, exercise your leadership by introducing powerful questions that engage others. Take the risk to ask the "taboo" questions and explore both ideas and reactions to new realities. Notice when board members and senior officers are able and willing to carve out time to inquire together and discover possible scenarios from the signs and signals. When the questions startle everyone out of complacency *and* board members make the connection between the nature of the questions and governance, readiness is ripening.

- What are the "wake up" questions you wish board members would ask?

- What are the discussions you wish you and your board would have right now?

- What questions do officers fear most? What questions do board members fear the most?

Join Convinced Players Who Are On the Field

Is there a group of board members ready to lead the transition to the next stage? Dick Beckhard, guru of organizational change, used to say that trying to drive change alone was suicide and driving change with one other person was jumping off Lover's Leap; he recommended starting with five cohorts engaged in the change effort and growing the number. Small groups working in parallel accelerate buy-in. Leadership by the group is in effect. Partners provide protection, an expanded network to influence, and a more robust picture of reality. Apply the same principle to your board—identify the small group that can lead and help bring others along. Enlist and support a critical mass of board members (25% to 30%) who truly believe in the board's ability and need to transform.

- Do you know who around the board table is ready to work toward a new governance model?

- Do you know who among the senior managers is ready to work with the board to transform?

When all three elements are present—recognizing extraordinary pressures impacting the enterprise and its contexts, individuals identifying and questioning the implications of these pressures for the board, and one third or more members willing to engage in the board's evolution—a board is ready to engage in the developmental tasks of transformation.

- Are **you** and others ready to participate in the board's transformation when it means you may change as well?

Recognize and Ripen Readiness at Each Major Transition

Each transition along the Continuum of Conscious Governance requires the board to develop new capabilities and enlarge their view out the window. Each board starts with its unique profile and progresses at its own pace of learning and change. Tenured board members' memories of past transitions will also influence their readiness to begin again. Think through how you will ascertain the board's readiness and how you will maintain momentum.

How to Talk About These Ideas

Is it really necessary to spend all this time and energy on Readiness—can't we just get started and people will catch up with us?

"Yes, it's really necessary. We've got too much to lose if we try to force our board on the journey. Board transformation is a fundamental change in the work of the board and how they do it. Board members must enroll—sign their own names to the transformation journey—to ensure we will have enough motivation and persistence. Others are more likely to join the effort if they see their colleagues personally committed to the transformation.

If this were an incremental change—realigning committees or adding social time to the agenda—we would only need people to comply. That would need more management than leadership.

Becoming a Mindful Board is important enough for us to take the time to build the understanding, commitment and persistence among board members. We don't want to fail our duties to the organization. We want to start with as many members as possible in the boat, rowing in the same direction."

Is building readiness to transform the same for every board?

"There are aspects of building readiness that are the same. Your board has its own style and history, so the process will be both predictable and unique to your situation."

Is it important to convince others early on?

"Every board member needs information about the choices available. The best way to help others get comfortable with the path to the Mindful Board and the process of building readiness is to keep asking questions that help expand consciousness and heighten context intelligence."

What if we miss the signs and signals?

"Boards—as human systems—have a marvelous way of persisting in the face of challenges, mistakes and resistance. If you and your board miss some signs and signals, you can rest assured more will follow. This is why building the foundational disciplines is so important and helpful."

Prescient's Board Shows Early Signs of Readiness to Transform

In Part 1 you were introduced to Prescient. The organization is clearly at a critical moment in its history. Building readiness can take time, especially when a board transforms from a Consent Board to a Working Board. As you read what happened, look for signs the R-Factor is ripening.

Marc is board chair. Jim is CEO. George is a mindful board member. Zach is vice president of marketing. Kim is CFO. Bob, Charles, Harry, Sean, Sophia, and Suzanne are board members. The board retreat referenced below is described in Chapter 3, the ad hoc strategic planning group and executive session in Chapter 4.

Two Months after the Executive Session

It has been three months since the board retreat and two months since the called executive session. Board member concerns about Jim's leadership have died down quickly after that special session, especially since it was clear Jim and his team were taking the output from that group and developing new approaches to solving the market share problem.

As Marc drives to the board meeting, he wonders what might happen that morning. Board members, individually and collectively, have continued to voice their dissatisfaction with their committees as well as with the discussions at board meetings. He has been surprised by the number of phone calls and emails he has received. One day he encountered Bob at a civic organization's lunch and even Bob expressed his concerns that the board was not talking about the "right stuff."

Normally, he and Jim would confer about the board meeting agenda a few weeks ahead of time and subsequently send out the notice. The conversations at the retreat several months ago, as well as the subsequent discussions, have stayed with Marc. This time he suggested to Jim that they include George in the meeting planning. George, in turn, suggested they include either Suzanne or Sean.

Turning the corner into the parking lot, Marc smiles to himself, remembering his own reaction to the suggestion from George to include others. At the time he almost jumped in his seat. In the end, he invited Suzanne to be part of the conversation. Her reaction to the invitation was mixed—a tad surprised and unsure of "her place." Marc had to reassure her that he and the others were interested in her perspective.

The four of them met to discuss the board meeting agenda. After considerable debate, they agreed to start the meeting with an update from Zach, the vice president of marketing, followed by a longer full board discussion about the implications of the data. All board members would receive Zach's report ahead of time. The goal was to make the meeting more of a Q&A session than a lecture. This bold move (at least it felt bold to Marc and Jim) was certainly new to the Prescient board culture.

Eruptions nearly volcanic occur at the meeting

The meeting starts on time and nearly everyone is present. The friendly tone present at 9:00 a.m. soon disappears. After a brief welcome from Marc, Zach makes a short presentation referencing the report already in board members' hands. The bottom line is that in spite of recent efforts to make marketing changes, Prescient is still struggling to reclaim a strong place in the market. Competitors and new entrants seem to be beating them at every turn.

Before the Q&A can even begin, the room erupts. Zach and Jim find themselves facing a hail of questions from every direction. Tensions rise. After about 20 minutes, Sean raises his hand. "I am very concerned about what all this means for the future of Prescient. But I'm starting to wonder what we're missing. We don't seem to have a good grasp of all the variables."

Harry leans forward and nods. "I agree with you, Sean. How can we see what we are obviously not seeing clearly? We are dependent on Jim and Zach and the other officers to give us what we need. I'm wondering if this is smart."

The four members of the ad hoc strategic planning group—Bob, Suzanne, Charles and George—look at each other and around the room with concern on their faces. George wades in with, "I am now convinced we need more outside expert points of view about the market and our industry. Or for that matter, perhaps we simply need guidance about how to navigate this slow growth economy. It's as if we are in a bubble and are afraid to look outward."

Silence follows. Marc steps in. "Good. Let's move forward. Jim, you and the team—with the ad hoc group—need to keep focused on evaluating the strategic plan and the effectiveness of your initiatives. In the meantime, we need to identify a speaker for our next board meeting. And, I want each committee chair to send me and Jim an email within the coming week spelling out what kind of external environment information or data your committee needs right now. Oh, and I would encourage you to poll your committee members before you send me that note!"

Marc calls George, of course, right after the board meeting

"Ok, I followed your advice and we had a fire storm. What the heck happened? And what am I supposed to do next?" shouts Marc into the phone.

George takes a deep breath and responds. "Marc, I thought it was actually a great meeting. Did you hear how many new questions were being asked? I particularly liked Sophia's question about how many other organizations in our industry are having similar problems. Notice we don't know the answer to that question. Then when Charles suggested that perhaps our internal operational business model is out of date. This is great stuff! The board is engaged! People are asking provocative questions. And, I get the sense more of our colleagues are thinking about the external context we are dealing with."

"Fine, fine," mutters Marc, "but you're not answering my question about what comes next."

"What comes next is we keep doing what we've started. Your suggestions and requests at the end of the meeting were very helpful. I think we'll learn a lot. We have to keep including others as we plan these meetings. Even though I suspect right about now you're ready to go back to the old way of setting agendas." George waits for Marc's reaction.

Marc nods to himself. There is a pause in the conversation. "I have to keep Jim from quitting or losing key officers. Somehow we have to figure out how to have these kinds of discussions without turning them into fights. I'll call Jim and see when he's free next week. I think you should come with me to see him. We need to debrief and plan."

"Great. I'm in." says George. "Oh, and Marc, invite Suzanne and Sean, too." George hears muttering as Marc hangs up.

What is happening?

The Prescient board is sending strong signals of no longer being happy as a Consent Board. It has taken a while to get here. George's reflections about the meeting point a light on the power of new questions, greater engagement of everyone, and what appears to be the start of heightened context intelligence. These are early signs of readiness. Marc's attention to the immediate concerns while also attending to the dissatisfaction about committees and board meeting discussions point to his ability to sense there are big changes afoot.

There is certainly fearless engagement at that board meeting! You can hear the genuine care for the individuals and the relationships between the board and senior management. George continues to coach Jim and Marc about the board meeting agendas, and is successful in drawing in others. Readiness is ripening.

Chapter 7

Recast the Limits:
Transform from Consent Board to Working Board

When we quit thinking primarily about ourselves and our own self-preservation, we undergo a truly heroic transformation of consciousness.

— Joseph Campbell, author of *"The Hero with a Thousand Faces"*

Be the Architect of Your Board's Transformation

Transforming all the way from a Consent Board to a Mindful Board may seem daunting. It is highly unlikely your board will make that kind of leap in a single bound; you move your board one stage at a time. While the path has common features, transformation is an intensely personal process that is never quite the same from board to board.

Just as architects use design principles as the starting point for their creativity, we invite you to envision how you will apply these action ideas to your board's journey. You will walk the path in your own way. Each successful move from one stage to the next builds the board's capabilities and skills to transform.

Get Started and Keep Moving with a Transition Plan

Keep your eye on essential ingredients as you develop your board's transition plan and/or approach. This can be a formal written plan, or a set of guiding principles which a committee or task group can use to lead the transition and transformation.

See clear evidence of readiness to transform to move forward. Use the model we describe in Chapter 6 to gauge readiness.

Employ the six tools to launch the transition and then to push forward. You will employ the tools in two steps. (Chapter 4 defines the tools.)

"Flip the switch" with a few tools to ignite the process. Decide which tools best fit your board's situation. For example:

- Choose two or three tools that give you the most "lift" or leverage to move quickly. Very often the tool that offers high impact is an intentional change in the design of board meetings (a key structure) along with changes in expectations of members during conversations at meetings (deliberations as a tool).

- If the context indicates you cannot afford too many mishaps, select tools you can work on without a lot of fanfare until the board and officers adjust to and enroll in the process.

- You can trust your selection of tools when the changes line up with the next stage on the path and the results are pulling the board forward. You have unleashed the energy and power available.

As we describe each of the three major transitions, we offer some suggestions about tools to select first so that you can see how the process works. You will need to make choices based on your board, organization, and the context.

Second, you "power up" by fully engaging all six tools (tasks, purpose, deliberations, structures, relationships, membership). This is how to get past the points where the effort can stall out. When you "power up to transform," you are orchestrating changes within all six elements. At this point the elements are super-tools that make it possible to take the final steps from transition to transformation. Significant changes can occur in succession, so be prepared for a boost in momentum. You will experience a sense of chaos while the new order of governance begins to emerge.

Develop and apply the six disciplines. As board capabilities grow from stage to stage, members' understanding of each discipline expands and mastery of the practice continues to develop. Draw on the disciplines individually and collectively as you make changes. Use the disciplines as diagnostic indicators of success or stress.

In Chapters 7, 8 and 9 we highlight the *discipline of reflection* to point to how to use the disciplines during the transition from one stage to the next. You will use all the disciplines and will need to determine how best to use each in your particular situation.

Need to refresh your understanding? Chapter 3 describes the six disciplines central to Conscious Governance. Chapter 4 describes each of the six elements and how they become tools—including how they transform along the continuum of Conscious Governance. Chapter 5 explores how to become a mindful board member.

From Our Case Files:

The executive team had expended countless hours with their board in a 12-month comprehensive due diligence process. The acquisition was in the center of the public's eye. The officers and board members were excited about the possibility but already exhausted before the deal was completed. Three months after the acquisition was official and their integration plan was initiated, the CEO called us to "Rescue me and my team. We are acting crazy." Officers had begun to speak pointedly at one another, or worse, to withhold information. Some stopped coming to meetings using workload as their excuse. They were terrible role models for leading the integration.

After an hour with the powerful question, "How well are we providing a role model for leading our integration plan?" we heard evidence that the power gradient had shifted significantly in the officer group. New officers had joined the executive team from the acquired entity—without earning their position—and resident officers had shifted in importance to the CEO. None of these relationship changes had been acknowledged but they were creating catastrophic consequences that rippled throughout the organization. Our long-standing relationship with the resident officers created a safe space that allowed us to make quite clear the shifts that had occurred (without naming specific people). Individuals talked about what they personally had lost and gained from the acquisition. The CEO explained why certain functions were now in the foreground with him.

At the board meeting the next month, the CEO presented "Lessons Learned So Far." When he explained the shift in power gradient, the board sighed in recognition. They had been struggling with their own reorganization to align with the acquisition and seen early warning signs in their own interactions.

The board members and officers who are committed to the transformation play a key role in normalizing reactions and listening to concerns. *Mindful board members and officers can model the disciplines of self-awareness, trustworthiness and reflection as they listen to the group. Apply expanded consciousness, fearless engagement, and leadership by the group as the board embraces change.*

No two transformations are exactly alike. Make this uniquely yours.

Leading the Move from Consent Board to Working Board

Let's look at the evidence of readiness followed by recommended steps to move from the Consent Board stage to the Working Board stage.

 Look up! This transition is not for the faint of heart

The move from Consent Board to Working Board is the most difficult transition because of the magnitude of the shift in the board's work and identity. Board members must shift from deferential detachment to greater knowledge of the core business (operations) and more director engagement in board tasks. Long-standing beliefs grounded in hierarchical models of executive authority, patronage (of all types), and formal power structures permeate the Consent Board. Every dimension of their governance model—board purpose, leadership, decision-making, relationships and much more—is challenged when facing the transition from Consent Board to Working Board.

See Evidence of Readiness

Look for the Very Early Signals

At this first transition point **dissatisfaction** shows up around:

- The amount of information and quality of that information senior management shares with the board about internal operations and enterprise performance.

- The degree of deference the board gives to the chair and the CEO's agenda in the face of challenges to the enterprise or the industry.

- The general way the board operates. This can be heard in criticisms of in-group/out-group dynamics, structure of board tasks, board meeting agendas, and the lack of tolerance for disagreement and dissent.

The board is looking for the source of its discontent and concern. *Cause-seeking* often points outward to the CEO and/or senior officers. Increased strain between the board and the CEO and senior officers is palpable but talked about privately. Members may be discontented with the board chair, but in this first transition the CEO, the central leader, is the most likely the target. The CEO's competency or behaviors or some aspect of the CEO's agenda can become the "call to action" by the board. The board's second target may be internal or external constituents who are "making things difficult."

Listen for Heightened Context Intelligence, Productive Inquiry and Committed Members

How do you know when readiness to transform has taken hold?

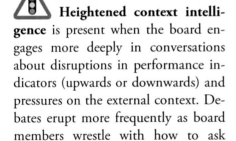 Heightened context intelligence is present when the board engages more deeply in conversations about disruptions in performance indicators (upwards or downwards) and pressures on the external context. Debates erupt more frequently as board members wrestle with how to ask questions that go deeper into an issue. Here are examples:

> We use our term "cause-seeking" rather than "blaming" to emphasize the intention to discover and understand the source of the disagreement and concern. Cause-seeking is both an intellectual and emotional response.

Board members criticize the background information provided around proposed strategic/operating plan issues or significant changes in how the enterprise is managed. This is perceived as new and "out of character." Board members express fear of not meeting fiduciary responsibilities because of the perceived gap.

Individual directors and the whole board ask specifically for more comprehensive information about operations and the marketplace and more time for discussion at board meetings.

Provocative articles are shared among board members who are seeking insights into the industry or economy.

A small group of directors emerges as informal leaders by demonstrating their willingness to take risks and offer new or opposing views on hot issues. In this first transition, this early sign of readiness is often tentative. Challenging management may still happen outside of the boardroom, but everyone hears about it in the end.

Take One Step at a Time

To heighten context intelligence board members will most likely need more data and information. Having adequate and convincing data to stretch the board's perspective may present a challenge, especially if the data did not come from the CEO. Be judicious in how far you ask members to go outside the boundaries of their comfort. Take one step at a time.

Productive and provocative inquiry is occurring with increasing frequency.

In the transition from Consent Board to Working Board, these signals are quite specific and are usually initiated by individuals but may be spontaneous in the group. Here are examples:

- Board members who have historically relied on management's interpretation of the external data start asking new and provocative questions about the external and internal contexts before agreeing with management perspective.

- In addition to questions about strategy and operations, new questions start to emerge about what is expected of board members in meetings and between meetings.

- Board members increasingly raise disquieting questions about the state of the industry and competition.

Asking precise or exposing questions is counter cultural on a Consent Board. Board members and officers will be challenged to not get defensive or overwhelmed by the questions. Another challenge is to not overreact to the gaps in data or knowledge that may be uncovered.

A group of committed board members lend their strong voice to enroll others in the need for transformation. Look for signals such as these:

- More board members are speaking up in general and engaging in discussions.

- Individuals start pushing to redesign agendas, meeting schedules, and other structures associated with the Consent Board.

- Committee chairs start exercising more freedom to set their meeting agendas.

The small group of committed members must be inclusive and gather consensus on the necessity of their transformation. If they push too hard or too fast, the committed group can erase any signs of readiness and reinforce others' resistance, especially from members accustomed to a Consent Board.

If you are not sure you are hearing and seeing signs of readiness, ask:

- Are the questions asked in plenary sessions pulling the board away from the consent agenda into new areas of inquiry?

- Are some board members calling for board reorganization in order to better support the enterprise and fulfill fiduciary responsibilities?

Watch For Signals to Slow Down

The board is probably not ready to transform into a Working Board when:

- Most of the board members like being a Consent Board and see no reason to change.

- The mental models around power, authority and the board-CEO relationship are fixed in traditional hierarchy and are so tightly bounded there is little tolerance for change.

- The board chair and/or CEO complain that the board is "micromanaging" and block questions and discussions.

- Board leadership or management express a desire to do things differently because it is considered "best practice" or recommended by the industry association, but in truth board members do not really want anything to change.

- Pressures on the enterprise are viewed by board members and senior management as transient rather than mission-critical.

Whether you use a formal or informal methodology to assess readiness, the goal is to understand the motivators and challenges to transformation. No set of conditions is ever perfect; the question is whether or not there is adequate commitment to move forward.

> **If you find yourself alone in believing it's time to transform, keep building the three attributes of readiness. Find at least one other person to work with you.**

Employ the Tools

For the Consent Board, the transition to Working Board is distinguished by the challenge to:

- open up tightly held roles and boundaries between the board, the board chair and the CEO;

- include everyone around the table in deliberations without pre-determined outcomes; and,

- embrace the possibility that new structures and capabilities are required because that is what is best for the organization.

To start the transition from Consent Board to Working Board, you will choose tools depending on pressures from the external and internal contexts, the quality of the board's relationships (inside the board and between the board and others), and the nature of deliberations. The elements are described in Chapter 4. To determine where to start, consider the key questions about each element:

Tasks: What commands the board's focus and attention in meetings and outside conversations?

Purpose: Why does this board exist? What is the deep, abiding purpose or value of this board?

Deliberations: What best describes the quality of deliberations and decision-making? Where do deliberations happen? What controls are in place and who manages the controls?

Structures: What are the most influential board structures and mental models? How is leadership, as a part of the board's culture, understood and enacted at this stage? How do practices and processes reflect what we believe about governance and leadership?

Relationships: What distinguishes the quality of relationships inside the board and between the board and senior leadership, customers, community leaders, regulators, etc.?

Membership: What is important about membership and being a member at this stage? What are the formal and informal expectations of board members in meetings?

Identify two of the elements as your starting point. We have some suggestions for you to consider so you can see how this works.

Flip the Switch to Start the Transition to Working Board

Start with changes in *structures and membership;* make changes that clearly reflect a Working Board. Disturb members who are comfortable with a Consent Board out of their complacency. These are board members who need direct experience of the value in making the transition. Use the disciplines of self-awareness and reflection as you monitor progress.

To make the tools work for you, use strategies such as:

Stretch Structures

There are several ways to *stretch the structures* and pull forward towards the Working Board. For example, use executive sessions to open up topics previously forbidden. Redesign the board meeting agenda to include more time for discussions on new topics and enlist others to participate in designing the meeting. As new committees are formed to reflect enterprise operational realities, ask committees to develop annual work plans. The plans will increase members' knowledge of how each committee's work reflects enterprise operational realities.

Leadership as a structure also needs to be stretched. Distribute leadership responsibilities more broadly than the four traditional positions: chair, vice chair, chair of finance, and chair of governance. *Practicing leadership by the group*—not leadership by the chosen few—can make a positive difference in the success of this launch.

Break down membership traditions and introduce new ones

Redefine membership expectations with the intention of bringing in skilled directors who are not socially tied to the CEO or board chair. In doing so, establish and implement term limits if your board does not currently have them. Be sure to include a discussion of the board's vision and intentions in new director orientation. Reinforce the importance of everyone's participation by assigning mentors or "board buddies" for new members to help them understand their contribution to the transformation.

Organize a Group for Action and Reflection

Commission a work group to orchestrate the change. These are members ready and willing to roll up their sleeves and get to work. The work group brings recommendations for specific actions to the full board for endorsement. This is the group who will put together the "flip the switch" action plan and the "power up" completion of that plan. With guidance from the board chair or executive committee, the group assesses readiness to transform, brings reflections on progress, and attends to member engagement as changes are enacted.

When the R-Factor is present changes to structures and membership are more than fixes on the margins. You can see how combining visible new structures that energize the group with the weightier task of establishing new expectations of members and changing membership traditions can keep momentum going.

Power Up to Transform into a Working Board

Use All the Tools:
Purpose+Tasks+Structures+Relationships+Membership+Deliberations

Once changes are underway inside structures and membership, *create high-impact changes in purpose, tasks, relationships, and deliberations*—all at the same time. As you consider the suggestions below imagine how the cumulative effect pulls the board forward.

Bundle these actions so that you are changing more than one thing at time. Here are a few examples of strategies:

Make Changes in Purpose and Tasks Explicit

Explicitly link purpose to the tasks—what the board spends its time on in meetings—to illuminate the difference between Consent Board and Working Board. Talking about purpose can be ambiguous and difficult, so design a board retreat around a big question such as, "How do we best support the enterprise, given the context and direction?" (Retreats also strengthen relationships.)

Craft a vision statement for the board that articulates the revised purpose and what that new purpose means for board tasks. Nothing will bring home the difference between a Consent Board and a Working Board more than committing the intention to paper. Use an ad hoc task group to figure out the process for doing this, invite a board member to facilitate it, and put the final vision statement at the top of every board meeting agenda for one to two years.

From Our Case Files:

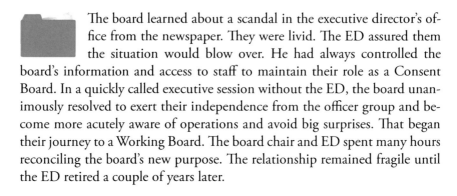

The board learned about a scandal in the executive director's office from the newspaper. They were livid. The ED assured them the situation would blow over. He had always controlled the board's information and access to staff to maintain their role as a Consent Board. In a quickly called executive session without the ED, the board unanimously resolved to exert their independence from the officer group and become more acutely aware of operations and avoid big surprises. That began their journey to a Working Board. The board chair and ED spent many hours reconciling the board's new purpose. The relationship remained fragile until the ED retired a couple of years later.

Change Structures to Enliven Deliberations and Strengthen Relationships

Use board retreats—one special structure—to launch transitions. Retreats are great tools for connecting the enterprise goals to board performance. Choose a facilitator carefully, making sure s/he understands the vision and the nature of the transition. Use small group break outs to build relationships. Experiment with different types of conversations and deliberations within the safety of the retreat.

From Our Case Files:

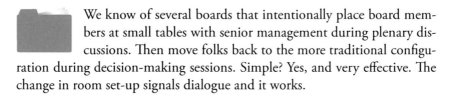

We know of several boards that intentionally place board members at small tables with senior management during plenary discussions. Then move folks back to the more traditional configuration during decision-making sessions. Simple? Yes, and very effective. The change in room set-up signals dialogue and it works.

Bring outside speakers into regular meetings to share information about critical issues facing the industry, and/or assign committees to be researchers who then make the presentation. This expands consciousness and generates a flow of new information that enlivens deliberations.

Set up the board's regular meeting room in a way that facilitates more dialogue, not less, and experiment with assigning seats so that new combinations of directors are sitting with each other. Shake up the environment!

One of our colleagues sets up his board meeting space into small clusters of tables organized as a chevron. He avoids the big square or rectangle and brings people closer to each other. While this may seem awkward, we've tried it and it creates a whole new sense of "working together" not just "listening together."

As you create new ways to energize the dialogue, be sure to spend dedicated time discussing and agreeing to "ground rules" or "operating norms" that include behaviors and values.

Most boards ask for some social time before the formal meeting starts. Retreats offer time for social interactions. Gathering for dinner the evening before is most common and often has a topic for discussion but no decisions.

Develop and Apply the Disciplines

Use the discipline of reflection to recognize when things go wrong.

Sometimes the best planned transitions go wrong and the board is off track or has slid backwards. Draw on all the disciplines (self-awareness, trustworthiness, reflection, expanded consciousness, leadership by the group, and fearless engagement) to regain balance and direction. Reflection draws on self-awareness and trustworthiness and makes it easier to discuss what went wrong.

Usually the "oops" is obvious—a committee is frustrated by lack of meaningful work, board members don't like the new agenda format, or agreed-upon changes have been summarily dropped. When the board chair signals openness to feedback and reflection, it is easier to name the "oops" out-loud.

Executive sessions can help restart the process by reflecting on what has gone awry. The board chair can pose the powerful question to jump start the conversation: "I am curious about our discussion of the budget. You all got very quiet. I would like to hear your thoughts. What happened?"

When things go wrong, or not perfectly, adapt. The greatest risk when this happens is giving up. So persevere.

Sample statements that show "something went wrong" in this transition:

- "We spend too much time in the weeds and get in the way of the people paid to run this place."

- "We've put the CEO and officers on the defensive. You can feel their resistance."

- "We don't have enough time in plenary to work through committee recommendations."

- "Too much process and not enough meat."

Convert these from stop signs to "pay attention signals" by exercising the disciplines and affirming the value of moving forward.

See Success—Big and Small

Reflection also helps you see progress. The transition from Consent Board to Working Board draws on systems thinking. You are changing and transforming the interconnected elements that make up the board's Conscious Governance system. Board work and interactions will go through awkward phases. At times it can be difficult to see or appreciate success as a result. Consider these ideas.

- Ask two or three board members to put together an annual statement of board performance and progress towards becoming a Working Board. The small group will engage in reflection and self-awareness. The document is for board-only and should be treated as confidential. The report will bring successes to the foreground and point to next steps. It also will speak to how the board members, individual and collectively, applied the disciplines to support the transition. Putting together an annual statement of this nature reinforces the value of intentional change efforts supported by the practice of expanded consciousness, fearless engagement and leadership by the group.

- Other board members may play a different role in the transition from Consent Board to Working Board. The role of the chair and/or vice chair of the Transition Team is twofold: to help the work group identify "quick wins" early on to gain momentum and to keep the ultimate goal in mind as work progresses. The action strategies typically are planned in one-year cycles which also guide the life cycle of some members of the group. There can be multi-year cycles depending on where the board is starting from and the desired stage. Members with specific expertise may be enlisted for the longer cycles. The Transition Team membership is dynamic and requires both stability and flexibility.

Manage the Momentum

Anyone who has lived through a significant change in personal or work life knows momentum matters. When it feels to members that progress is slagging, increase the efforts. When officers are complaining or celebrating the changes, make sure the board is informed. Establish new feedback mechanisms about the changes and ideas for next steps. This can include meeting evaluations, committee performance evaluations, and whole board self-evaluations. To avoid "same old stuff" syndrome, customize the questions. *Lean into self-awareness and reflection* when crafting the questions.

Expect this transformation to take one to two years. Once you reach Working Board and demonstrate the board's ability to sustain this stage, the next transition is not as disturbing because the board, CEO and senior management—as a learning system—carry forward the institutional memory of the transformation.

Moving along the Conscious Governance continuum is a cumulative process: The fiduciary oversight skills of the Consent Board are brought forward into the Working Board. The new skills, disciplines and capabilities mastered by the Working Board are carried forward into the next stage.

Prescient's Board Enjoys Life as a Working Board

The Prescient board made the transition to Working Board and is now about one year into this new reality. The transformation process has been hard work, but a strong group of members has kept the changes moving forward. Such a process does not come without reactions. One of those reactions can sometimes be board member resignations, as is the case for Prescient's board. The loss of a valued member also opens up an opportunity.

One year into life as a Working Board

The volcanic eruptions at board meetings have given way to deeper conversations as Marc, Jim, George and others have worked diligently to improve board and committee meetings. By adjusting a variety of structures, board members have found it easier to engage fully in discussions and dared to raise questions previously forbidden. At the same time, board member expectations have been reviewed and updated. This second major step has involved both the board and the senior officers. Making changes to membership has resulted in a set of mutual expectations that have started to build a new partnership. Nearly everyone is pleased—but not everyone.

"Marc," says Harry, "it's time for me to resign from the board." Marc isn't completely surprised. Over the past year Harry has become increasingly quiet at meetings and often has left before the meeting concluded.

Marc looks at Harry over the lunch table. They have known each other for many years, and together have been serving on the Prescient board for over ten years. "Harry, can you tell me what's on your mind?"

Harry shifts in his seat, rearranges the coffee cup, and clears his throat. "I appreciate all you and the others have been doing to make our board meetings more productive. I certainly think we've made progress. I am just not cut out for these intense conversations and constant questioning of our strategy and direction. I'm not saying we shouldn't be asking the questions, but I don't believe I can contribute anything of value. After all, I'm older than most of the others and my approach to these things is different."

Marc watches his friend with regret and understanding. "Is there anything I can do to make your experience on this board better?"

"No, Marc. I felt comfortable with our old model. This new approach is certainly lively, but it's not me."

Marc accepts Harry's resignation, though not easily. Several weeks later, after considerable reflection on the situation, Marc realizes an important seat on the board is now open. Harry had chaired a variety of committees over the years and is seen as a key member. He wonders how others will react to Harry's resignation. He knows Jim will not be pleased. He also trusts that other board members will understand Harry's discomfort and will honor his decision.

On the morning before the governance committee meeting, Marc is gathering up his papers when he realizes that whoever they recruit next will matter more than in the past.

What we see happening now

Transformation brings many changes on many levels. Clearly this board is learning how to use deep conversations to guide deliberations. At the same time, Marc is navigating the human side of the process as much as the formal governance side. This is a dynamic that will continue as Prescient's board transforms yet again.

ھ

Let's go to the second transition—from Working Board to Strategic Board!

Chapter 8

Expand the View from the Balcony:
Transform from Working Board to Strategic Board

What we need to do is always lean into the future; when the world changes around you and when it changes against you - what used to be a tail wind is now a head wind - you have to lean into that and figure out what to do because complaining isn't a strategy.

— Jeff Bezos, CEO Amazon.com

Get ready to move from Working Board to Strategic Board

Once again you will keep an eye on essential ingredients of a transition and transformation plan. You will:

- See clear evidence of readiness to transform.

- Employ the tools in two steps.

- Develop and apply the six disciplines.

Leading the Move from Working Board to Strategic Board

This move does not shake the board's foundation of underlying beliefs like the move from Consent to Working board does. However, the move from Working Board to Strategic Board has its own significant barriers. You must make a compelling case for strategic governance.

 Look out the window! Think future and look beyond the parking lot!

Strategic governance, a hallmark of the Strategic Board, builds the capability to anticipate, interpret and act on ambiguous external factors from multiple sources; it is meaning-making at a new breadth of deliberations. Strategic governance demands faith in imagination and "out of the box thinking." When internal and external contexts are changing or the industry faces a paradigm shift, disentangling the threads requires analytics, creativity and intuition. The Strategic Board values the tasks of analysis and imagining as it seeks to understand and leverage the anticipated shifts in the industry.

Here's where we've been and where we're going: Chapter 3 introduces the six disciplines as central to Conscious Governance. Chapter 4 describes each of the six elements and how they become tools—including how they transform along the continuum of Conscious Governance. Chapter 5 explores how to become a mindful board member. Chapter 6 defines readiness to transform. Chapter 7 outlines the move from Consent Board to Working Board.

The move to Strategic Board is a transformation in the quality and content of the board's thinking, deliberations, and the ability to work in a longer time frame with senior officers. Board members and officers are collaborating to anticipate the future while managing the present.

See Evidence of Readiness

Look for the Very Early Signals

At this transition point, the board's **dissatisfaction** shows up around:

- The board committee structure creating silos and getting in the way of seeing "the big picture."

- Members calling for more time and focus on long-term strategic questions. This may also take the form of complaints that the strategic plan is in truth just an annual or multi-year operational plan, not a strategy. Criticisms may also focus on how industry, economic and societal trend information is analyzed and shared with the board.

- The board questioning the meeting agenda, including dissatisfaction with a lack of new insights and ideas coming out of deliberations. This may include concerns about what management presents, the way conversations are facilitated, or the lack of industry (and beyond) trend information.

Cause-seeking usually points first at board leadership—including the chair, board officers, and committee chairs (and sometimes informal leaders). Pay attention if complaints about the chair's style of guiding meetings start to gain energy in sidebar conversations or even in executive sessions. The CEO and senior officers are still common sources of dissatisfaction. Remember, transformation is not about the person—it's about context, purpose and practices.

Work to get a constructive focus on the board's governance practices and not blaming specific individuals. The issue is not "bad board" but limited consciousness; direct attention to the strategic issues facing the enterprise and the board's concerns about guiding the system. Refocus on the big picture.

Listen for Heightened Context Intelligence, Productive Inquiry and Committed Members

Heightened context intelligence is present when conversations start to include or respond to marketplace dynamics with more sophistication and nuanced understanding of the potential implications. Industry analysts talk about future uncertainty across the industry. Directors bring their research and interpretations into board deliberations. Analysts' sense of disquiet carries more weight with the Strategic Board.

Board members and senior managers debate how to capitalize on breakthroughs and/or breakdowns among competitors, similar industries, and across sectors. They attend conferences to learn more about emerging trends.

In the midst of the angst, some board members see a fortuitous opportunity on the horizon to meet an unmet need or serve a new market, new constituents, or a new group of stakeholders. They raise questions, however, as to whether or not the board is able to enlist the CEO and officers.

Productive and provocative inquiry raises new possibilities that startle board members and officers.

- Questions pop up about long-term strategy and direction at every meeting. Inside and outside the boardroom, trustees are asking whether the strategic plan reflects a "real strategy."

- New questions are predictive indicators and demands for outcome measures that capture the long-term impact of the activities associated with the plan beyond the plan's end date.

- Questions are more obviously connected to disruptions in the sector, the market, the industry and beyond than ever before.

Questions generated may require research and outside expertise. Some board members may have little patience for pursuing long term opportunities.

Committed board members start raising questions openly about the board's capabilities. Look for signals such as these:

- Officers and/or board members complaining the board is micromanaging and missing the "big stuff." Some members are afraid of surprises from the marketplace.

- Board members and officers voice dissatisfaction with the board's structure; they describe it as cumbersome, entrenched and lacking in strategic focus.

- Board members question the content of board meetings and deliberations as too operational and not focused on the big picture.

A trustee in higher education said to us recently, "I don't know how to connect the dots between the committees. How can I know the real big picture for this institution?" Committees on Working Boards are functional units and are designed to reflect how the organization is structured. They are not designed to connect the dots. Board members are generally left alone to grasp how one area impacts another in the elusive big picture. This trustee's comment was a clarion call for transformation to Strategic Board.

Look for Collaboration

You may also see signs of readiness when the committed board members demand collaboration. Committee chairs start arranging joint meetings with other committees to discuss overlapping strategic or operational issues.

Board members want less time spent on committee meetings and more time in plenary sessions engaged with each other as a whole group.

Board members raise questions about the impact and effectiveness of the current strategy and want more dynamic metrics that capture interdependent outcomes.

> **If you are not sure you are hearing and seeing signs of readiness at this transition point, ask:**
>
> • Are the deliberations going deeper and taking the board into new aspects of the organization's strategic challenges?
>
> • Are board members calling for changes in how the board spends its time in order to respond more effectively to changing external contexts?

Watch for Signals to Slow Down

The board is probably not ready to transform from a Working Board to a Strategic Board when:

• The board chair and CEO block efforts to redesign meetings.

• Discussion of what it means to be a Strategic Board keeps getting rescheduled to another date.

• Board members resist considering how trends in other industries are relevant.

• Early attempts at strategic thinking are labeled "a waste of time" or are purview of the executive team.

Despair not: if the board isn't quite ready, the seeds of possibility have been planted. If readiness isn't quite there, find someone to work with you and keep moving. If, on the other hand, readiness is truly present and the board is ready to take action, let's look at how to transform into a Strategic Board.

Employ the Six Tools

Grasping the distinctions between Working Board and Strategic Board can scramble the brain for some board members—particularly those who are very comfortable in the realm of operational management or who run transactional businesses. Becoming a Strategic Board means you leave behind familiar structures and the predictability of meeting agendas. You enter new territory.

The second transition to Strategic Board is marked by the need to:

- articulate a clear vision and rationale for what it means to become a Strategic Board;

- create opportunities to get feedback from outsiders about the board's ability to govern strategically and elevate their questions and discussions to see more broadly from "the balcony;" and

- adjust interactions and behaviors to realize a collaborative partnership with the CEO and officers while respecting roles.

> Imagine yourself on a balcony. You can see what's happening on the ground. And, as you go up to higher balconies, your view of the landscape and the horizon expands. As you and your board move along the Conscious Governance path, you are moving to higher balconies.

If the R-Factor is present, you're ready to start. We have a few suggestions for you to consider.

Flip the Switch to Start the Transition to Strategic Board

Activate Purpose + Structures + Deliberations

Launch the transition to Strategic Board with changes in *purpose, structures and deliberations.* Once again use strategies that bundle changes among the three elements.

Bring Clarity to the New Purpose

Craft a working definition of strategic governance for your board. Distinguish among strategic planning, strategic thinking and strategic governance. Articulate the role of the board and officers in each. Some members may find this a dubious intellectual exercise, but it pays off when the board is wrestling with messy strategy issues. There will be a shared understanding of what is needed—planning, thinking or governance. Then, put the accepted definition of strategic governance on the back of name tent cards so each person sees the definition when she/he sits down at a meeting.

From Our Case Files:

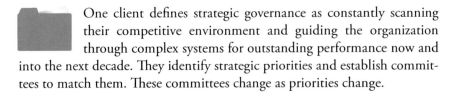 One client defines strategic governance as constantly scanning their competitive environment and guiding the organization through complex systems for outstanding performance now and into the next decade. They identify strategic priorities and establish committees to match them. These committees change as priorities change.

Experiment with ways to enhance capabilities associated with strategic governance (creativity, insight, imagination, systems-thinking, and integrative thinking). It helps to appropriately shrink the traditional firewall between the board and outsiders to ensure that new and useful ideas flow into the boardroom.

As all this is happening, engage executives and key stakeholders in imagining the enterprise in 10 - 20 years, a long-term vision. Identify changes the board would need to sponsor or implement for the organization to realize that vision and what changes the board itself must embrace to guide that envisioned future.

Leverage Structures Creatively

Make an effort to *intentionally bring committees together* in combined meetings to work on a shared goal. Arrange conference calls among related committees between board meetings. If that is too cumbersome, create ad hoc task groups that include board members who do not usually work together or don't know each other very well to wrestle with issues or ideas that do not neatly fall into your board's committee structure. Assign emerging board leaders to chair them.

Rewrite committee charters so that they fulfill fiduciary tasks, assure appropriate knowledge of operations, and explicitly align with the organization's strategic priorities.

A strategic group brings energy, creativity and project management skills to their endeavor. At each transition point it is vitally important to authorize or empower the group. Authorization and empowerment can come from the chair, the executive committee, the governance committee, a combination, and from consensus of the whole board.

Carve out time at a board meeting to reflect on how board members, the CEO and senior leaders are experiencing the transition. This intentional pause is as important as getting the action steps completed.

Create Opportunities for Deliberations that Strengthen Relationships

Hold a working session where the board brings forward examples that compare operational questions and powerful questions that reflect the broader perspective from the Strategic Board balcony. Bring forward a real-time issue facing the enterprise as the content. Change the usual seating arrangements for the discussion.

Hold a learning retreat for board and senior leaders to think about the industry, economy, political or regulatory issues. Pre-work must be intellectually captivating. Have a skilled facilitator guide the learning process to form a robust strategy across the management-governance boundary.

Convene an annual conference with speakers and critical stakeholders from outside the organization to discuss industry trends or pressures arising from divergent social-economic-environmental issues and geo-political dynamics. Invite people from the industry and region to enrich the conversations.

Lean Into the Flip the Switch Starting Point

Select a starting point—consider the suggestions offered above for each transition. And make it your own. Keep it simple but be mindful in the intention, ultimately, to effect a transformation over time. You are the architect who sees the current and future states of the board's practice of governance.

Power Up to Transform into a Strategic Board

Use All the Tools:
Purpose+Tasks+Structures+Relationships+Membership+Deliberations

We once heard a board leader state with great emotion, "We can't be at the strategy level all the time!" How true. Becoming a Strategic Board is not about an obsessive focus on the strategic plan. It's about how board members think and act. It's about asking questions that pull the whole group beyond the walls of the organization and towards the future—doing more than solving today's dilemmas.

Align Strategies When You Power Up

The group leading the board's transformation may have to run to keep up with all that's going on. In the organization, several strategic initiatives are being implemented simultaneously. Leaders and managers are learning rapidly and applying their new insights. The board is in the "power up" phase for their transformation to govern the emerging organization. You and your colleagues are employing each of the six elements. A lot is going on—there are many moving parts in the governance system.

Your attention needs to be evenly divided between planning the board's transformation details and overseeing the overall impact of the strategic changes on the system. Be clear about what work belongs to the executive group and what belongs to the board to avoid double efforts or strained relationships. The two action plans—the organization's transformation plan for the executives to implement and one for the board's transformation—uplift a new set of specific, measurable and time-bounded objectives for each group. *Leadership by the group* expands its boundaries and matters more than ever at this transition point.

> **Be clear about what work belongs to the executive group and what belongs to the board to avoid double efforts or strained relationships.**

Infuse Board Tasks with Exciting Opportunities

Create experiences that get board members out of their chairs. Invite board members to attend industry conferences and regional economic forums with the officers. Arrange for board members to meet key customers previously unknown to them to hear their perspectives on the services or products as well as the industry. And meet with policy experts in your industry to hear their interpretation of what is occurring with regulations and the implications.

Continue to Shift Structures to Promote Dialogue

Use a half-day retreat or dinner meeting to engage in a conversation about social-economic-political-environmental trends around the world in industries *different from yours* and then ask board members to track the patterns and possible connections to your enterprise. Drawing from the retreat, put two provocative strategic questions on the board agenda to encourage thinking about an issue or pending decision in a new way. Start with, "What if…"

Raise Membership Expectations

This is always a challenge. *Recruit some new board members* with an aptitude for strategic thinking. Reinforce the new expectations through a transparent and intentional leadership development program for board members that emphasize stretching committees' perspectives and disentangling complex issues.

Enlist seasoned board leaders and bring into the circle of commitment new members and emerging leaders to continuously assess the transition plan and reflect on the apparent outcomes of your actions. Test the ideas in the current transition plan against the desired end state: will these actions build a transition bridge for transformation? That testing occurs through conversations with the board leadership, the CEO and officers, and with the board as a whole.

Develop and implement individual board member assessments that give both the board chair and the member an opportunity to discuss his/her effectiveness on a Strategic Board. Check to be the assessments that reflect the new attributes of the Strategic Board. And make sure new member orientation includes mentors and a feedback loop to the governance committee to ensure on-boarding fits the new stage.

Develop and Apply the Disciplines

Use Reflection to Recognize When Things Go Wrong

As with the first transition, you will again *practice the discipline of reflection* during the high and low points of the process. The "oops" happens in this transition when the group leading the transition gets ahead of the rest. They advance ideas or strategies when the rest of the board or executives aren't quite ready.

We witnessed this dynamic in real time when the governance committee of a board wanted to increase the complexity of the questions in plenary sessions but the pre-work didn't adequately prepare the directors. Committees were confused and frustrated because they didn't "get" the goal of building a shared view of their complex organization as a cutting-edge leader in its industry. The result was that the board rejected efforts to facilitate cross-committee discussions to create a systems view of the initiatives.

Lesson learned: Describe what you are doing and why; repeat several times; guide the discussions to a higher balcony. Point out the difference between the old way and new way when board members appear resistant, frustrated, impatient, or confused.

Statements made by board members and officers that show "something went wrong" in this transition:

- "What do you mean by 'strategic' anyway?"
- "What is a 'strategic balcony' question?"
- "I am not sure what questions we should be asking."
- "It's not realistic to think beyond 3 or 4 years."
- "Who is creating the strategy—the officers or the board?"

The "balcony perspective" is ambiguous as a big idea, but it is an important part of the Strategic Board identity. As the board moves along the continuum, the balconies or perspectives are higher and more inclusive because the horizon is extended. Imagine yourself on a balcony—you can still see the ground even as you see much more. You can appreciate the full context much better from a higher balcony.

To help board members feel confident about the transition to Strategic Board, employ various metaphors as appropriate. The balcony metaphor is one. You may use the airplane's altitude as a metaphor. Boards move their thinking and acting from 10,000 feet to 30,000 feet. Another metaphor is the view out the window. Consent Boards look out one window. The Working Board looks out a couple of windows. The Strategic Board is looking out multiple windows from different vantage points to see what is ahead. The idea is to create the picture that best works for your group of people.

Use Reflection to See Success—Big and Small

Persistence is the watchword of the transition. We are now in a zone of consciousness that asks board members to trust their ability to interpret data and see beyond the metrics to implications for the organization's future. Here are a few ideas:

- As in the first transition, write an annual statement of board performance and progress towards becoming a Strategic Board. Get feedback from officers on how the partnership is working. This is a board-only document and should be treated as confidential. It brings successes to the foreground and points to next steps.

- In the transition to Strategic Board, telling a memorable customer story about moving to the new perspective is compelling. Use the story to orient new members, calibrate current activities, and inspire forward movement.

The shift beyond traditional operational boundaries requires intelligence, creativity, and an ability to see patterns and trends.

Manage the Momentum with Data

To keep the pieces in motion without overwhelming the CEO, officers, board chair, committee chairs and everyone else, develop easy tools for board self-evaluation and apply them regularly.

Implement and Monitor

As with any planned development process, implementation and monitoring of progress constitute the feedback mechanism for improvement. *Use the board's capacity for conscious reflection.* Where is this board on the Conscious Governance continuum and what propels us forward? What are we experiencing as easy and exciting, and what's not working as well? What are we learning about ourselves?

Electronic surveys make the task manageable. Don't make it too complicated! The results might mean slowing down or speeding up. The key to any board self-evaluation is the follow-up discussion and action plan. Data collection without reflection and visible trustworthy actions will be wasted time and effort.

Annual operating plans and longer term strategic plans usually include metrics and progress reports. These can amplify performance—both internal operational performance and the board's performance. When reviewing progress against these plans, build a safe environment for board members and officers to voice their observations, concerns and hopes. And keep asking the question "Is our board evolving to meet the challenges of the enterprise?"

Prescient's Future and the Demand to Become a Strategic Board

Dramatic changes that occur simultaneously inside and outside the organization can startle the board awake. For Prescient's board, being a Working Board has been a lot of fun and productive. Disquieting questions are popping up. New players are shaking things up. The combination leads the board to wonder if it is working at the appropriate level.

The Players Start Changing—a New Line Up Emerges

For Marc, being the Prescient board chair is a great honor. He loves being chair. Granted, the past several years have been hard work and at times nerve-racking. For Marc that first board retreat—now over two years ago—was a key turning point. He had to lead differently and he had to enlist others to help navigate the pressures on Prescient and the tensions inside the board. Since then the partnership between the board, the CEO and officers have matured. Meetings are full of rich dialogue and all board members are engaged. Yet, he knows it is time for him to step down as board chair.

Marc calls George, who is chairing the governance committee, to tell him to get his committee working on finding a new board chair. The two of them have been talking about this possibility for quite some time. George acknowledges Marc's request and adds "This is an opportunity to look at the protocol to make sure the process is inclusive and transparent—if that's possible. Otherwise, we will risk sliding backwards." Marc agrees.

An opportunity to model the disciplines arises

The committee has indeed reviewed and revised the process they will use to bring forward a new slate of board officers. The whole board has had the opportunity to comment on the ideas and there has seemed to be comfort with the approach they would take. It certainly is far more inclusive than years back, when Marc was named board chair. Once the board figures out the process, the committee members are assigned board members to talk with and gather names. The list of suggestions is short and robust. George finds himself in a position where he needs to recuse himself from the nominations since his name has been suggested many times.

Everyone has agreed that voting on a slate would create more division than unity, so the governance committee has spent several hours reviewing the list (names recommended by board members), and asking these questions: What personal attributes and leadership qualities does our board need from the chair at this time? What are the major issues facing Prescient that the next board chair will need to help the organization and the board navigate?

After substantive deliberations, the committee has forwarded their recommendation to Marc and Jim. Marc quickly agrees. Shortly thereafter, at the next board meeting, the group agrees with the recommendations. George becomes the chair-elect. He will assume the chair role immediately after the annual meeting.

Once the vote is over and the dust settles George suggests it might be time to review the bylaws and update them. He has become aware that how board officers are selected and the evolving nature of committees and membership expectations give reason to such a task. Again, the board agrees. The governance committee goes to work.

More leadership changes—enter Dave, the new Chief Operating Officer

During the time Marc was considering his decision to step down as board chair, he brought Jim into his confidence. Jim in turn confided that he had decided to create the role of Chief Operating Officer. He wanted someone who could be groomed as his successor, and who would bring a level of strategic thinking and management much needed in the organization. "You know, Marc," said Jim, "you're not the only one who sees the handwriting on the wall. I'm figuring I have about three good years left. It's time for new ideas and new leadership. We are doing better, but Prescient's future requires a new approach. I'm just an old dog on the porch—someone who is still happy, by the way, but not foolish." Marc grinned at Jim.

Keeping his word, Jim informs the board of his decision to create and fill the new role. He asks several board members to participate in the interview process when it comes time to review the finalists. In the end, he hires Dave, who came to Prescient with significant depth of experience in turn-around efforts and bold strategic moves. Dave is quickly accepted by the team and the board. He is an excellent listener and shows his ability to connect what he is learning about the history and challenges to the opportunities he sees for the enterprise.

At board meetings, Dave respectfully asks much more provocative questions about strategy and Prescient's future. While some board members are disquieted, others are excited. At the celebration of Marc's leadership and completion of his term as board chair, Marc applauds Jim for his foresight in hiring Dave and states his expectations of everyone, "We can have a great future. I am counting on all of you to step up and create that future." Shortly thereafter, Dave enlists the senior team to work with him and George to figure out how the officers could help the board become more strategic in its deliberations.

Meanwhile, a new board member shakes things up

Harry's resignation from the board has been met with regret and recognition by many that the open seat generates an important dialogue about what the board needed from its members. The governance committee wrestles with the question at a lengthy committee meeting. George, as chair of the committee, brings forward the committee's ideas and the specific need to find candidates with strong strategic thinking skills. The board conversation leads to adding the importance of finding true global citizens who could help the board and senior managers understand the rapidly changing external contexts.

Sophia, who met Eliza at a global conference on innovation and business transformations, submits Eliza's name to the governance committee for consideration. After a relatively fast-tracked process of interviewing and considering her candidacy, the committee brings forward her name for approval. Both Marc and Jim enthusiastically endorse her as a potential board member. Eliza is delighted to be invited and dives into her board service at Prescient with high energy along with sharply focused and insightful questions always on the tip of her tongue.

Eliza is not your typical Prescient board member. For one thing, she brings a global perspective on many trends and issues that crisscross multiple industries and sectors, including Prescient's. She consults internationally and has lived and worked in five different countries. No one else around the table has such a wide and deep grasp of the emerging business and social issues. While some board members find her disconcerting, she demonstrates her willingness to learn about Prescient and honor its history. As Dave gets his feet on the ground, he finds a ready supporter in Eliza when it comes to strategy and direction. This newcomer phenomenon is, at the moment, welcomed by other board members. The multiplier effect of the new questions and increased energy prompt a conversation at a board meeting that takes everyone by surprise.

"How do we become strategic?"

Sean has long since been accepted and valued as a Prescient board member. His informal role of "wild card board member" shows up again when, at a planning meeting for the upcoming board meeting, he enters the conversation with his observation. "We're stuck. Just plain stuck. I listened to Eliza at the last meeting and realized we are not asking great questions. We're not even thinking beyond the next two years. We need to take our deliberations to a whole new level. Oh, and before you ask, I'm not sure how we do this but we need to figure it out." Marc and Jim stare at him with a look of amazement while also nodding. It happens that Zoe is at that meeting. She turns to Marc and says, "Marc, I know the next meeting is your last meeting. I think we're asking a lot of you, but can you help frame the challenge for the board? How do we become strategic? Would you be willing to?"

Marc answers without hesitation, "Absolutely. I agree. I'm with Sean. I have no idea how you all will get there, but I am confident you can figure it out. Let's keep talking."

What is happening now

The Prescient board is further along the path towards becoming a Strategic Board than they realize. The board and CEO are embracing new questions and striving to see the future from a much longer view than previously. Recognizing their "stuckness" is a clear sign they are well on their way to a new balcony. Marc's decision to step down as board chair could be either an opportunity or a distraction. We'll see what happens in the next installment.

You and your board have come a long way by this point.

Now… let's now look at the third transition—transformation from Strategic Board to Mindful Board!

Chapter 9

Focus on Impact:
Transform from Strategic Board to Mindful Board

Institutions need two kinds of leaders: those who are inside and carry the active day-to-day roles, and those who stand outside but are intimately concerned and who, with the benefit of some detachment, oversee the active leaders. These are the trustees. Trustees carry a critical leadership role that cannot be dispensed with. There should be only one requirement: he or she must be an able, dedicated servant-leader who will work hard to assure distinguished performance of the institution in trust.

— Robert Greenleaf, the founder of the servant leadership movement

You and your board have reached an extraordinary moment!

Once again you will keep an eye on the essential ingredients of a transition and transformation plan. You will:

- See clear evidence of readiness to transform.

- Employ the tools in two steps.

- Develop and apply the six disciplines.

Leading the Move from Strategic Board to Mindful Board

 Look out every window! Ready or not, here we come!

The transition to Mindful Board becomes possible when the board internalizes the expanded scope of accountability that comes with mastering the disciplines of expanded consciousness, leadership by the group, and fearless engagement. Trends and disruptions your board ignored before can become the catalyst for the Mindful Board.

See Evidence of Readiness

Look for the Very Early Signals

At the third transition point—Strategic Board to Mindful Board—**dissatisfaction** shows up in more subtle ways. Examples are:

- Discomfort with the apparent and unseen impact of decisions increases. Board members wonder about the impact of decisions on those outside of the immediate influence of the enterprise. Impact on the community economy or environment where a manufacturing plant is located is an example. Board's awareness may emerge as a result of unfortunate events cause either by the organization or by another within the industry or even beyond the industry.

- Board deliberations and decisions seem inadequate, lacking relevant data or wide enough perspectives. Board members may express this feeling because of increased awareness of the larger societal and global social-economic-political-environmental events on the industry and the enterprise.

- Concerns about complexity are tinged with concerns about deliberations. Some members keep saying there isn't enough time spent on the bigger picture while other members complain the board is ignoring the basics. This tension is part of the "space between" the two stages.

Cause-seeking does not have a clear target at this point, such as board leadership, the CEO or regulators. Rather, the board struggles to identify the source of their discomfort starting with themselves. Conversations are chaotic and unfocused because they have a sense of "everything is out of control."

The call to action can be addressing a specific policy or aspect of operations or trying to understand a disconcerting pattern of outcomes or emerging trends.

Listen for Heightened Context Intelligence, Productive Inquiry and Committed Members

Heightened context intelligence is present when big shifts, new paradigms or unexpected disruptions touch the industry, nation, global economy, or social networks. In boardroom conversations, topics now include, more than ever:

- Constituents who are demanding your organization change its way of operating.

- Key stakeholders demanding redirecting your investment portfolio to socially responsible and sustainable funds.

- Your industry or sector coming under fire for business practices. Regulators and politicians are forcing your organization to remedy consequences of accepted practices.

- Geo-political changes in other markets strongly impacting your organization's ability to do business ethically or safely. A committee may suggest working through affiliates to limit liability. The organization becomes a different entity with management stresses.

Productive and provocative inquiry needs skillful facilitation, especially at this transition point. Too many questions can overwhelm board members and stall their meetings. Provocative questions may cause anxiety and premature problem-solving.

- Board members describe a situation that is not directly connected to the organization and ask a series of "What if" questions.

- External experts provoke intense discussions on the actual performance and validity of the organization.

- The current long-range plan is challenged by board members as too parochial and socially unaware.

The board is ready to expand the boundaries of their consideration and will likely need to manage their meeting agendas closely as they develop the mindful disciplines.

⚠️ **Committed members are the small group that can easily move among the four contexts.** For others, changing contexts and implications is annoying.

- Committed members begin seeding their ideas with articles and reports that allow others to consider at their own pace the bigger possibilities or consequences being proposed.

- Board members want to hold an off-site strategy retreat with officers.

- Board members, thinking well into the future, ask more questions about new hires on the executive team.

As this occurs, relationships can be strained until the board knows how it will practice mindful governance. If you sense there is a readiness, the big question comes: **Where are we now on the continuum and why do we want to transform?** This is not a one-time question. Ask this question at each transition point and wait for the full board and the CEO and senior officers to answer. Also ask the question when the process seems rocky or the board feels stuck. Keep coming back to this powerful question. Then, lean in and move forward.

If you are not sure if you're hearing or seeing signs of readiness ask:

- Do members ask about impact of your products and services beyond the direct customers?

- Does the board have the patience and skills to go deep and broad into a strategic topic?

- Are some board members seeing connections between global, environmental, or political issues and the organization's goals?

Recognize Clear Signs to Slow Down

The board is probably not ready to transform from a Strategic Board to a Mindful Board when:

- A startling number of board members are talking about resigning.

- Officers are complaining they can't get the attention of the board on urgent matters.

- The board is unable to reach important conclusions on key matters.

Yes, the Process Will Be Messy

There is no way to avoid this reality: human systems undergoing transformational change make messes. The transformation from a Strategic Board into a Mindful Board is no exception. So be prepared for some mistakes, surprises, and fabulous leaps along the way. It is a journey!

Embrace What is Different This Time

The Mindful Board focuses beyond the formal strategy's horizon. The Mindful Board governs with shared ownership of the outcomes across multiple systems and the impact of its decisions over many years. The Mindful Board's depth of stewardship is far greater than that of any of the other stages. This profound shift brings the paradox of urgency paired with discernment. The transformation to Mindful Board catapults the board into a broader and deeper sense of responsibility. Mindful Boards courageously consider the known consequences and possible unintended consequences of decisions. The board can effectively manage fulfilling fiduciary responsibilities, but the mindset with which the board approaches core tasks has profoundly shifted.

> **Confused or stuck? Keep asking the question, "Why now?" Listen to the answer. Then lean in and move forward.**

Someone recently asked us if a global enterprise finds it easier to become a Mindful Board than smaller more locally focused organizations. Smaller organizations and large global enterprises have boards at every stage. Being "global" does not automatically make it easier to be a Mindful Board. Being a local or regional organization does not make it easier to be a Mindful Board. Making the transition from Strategic Board to Mindful Board is the same for everyone moving along the continuum: you make the integrated changes to get you there.

Each transition point has particular characteristics and challenges. In this third transition, these include:

- Conversations and deliberations focus less on information as a set of facts and focus more on how the depth of information and knowledge present in the room flows through the conversation. Because the transition is more intellectual and less about specific tasks, board members are stretched to broaden their thinking as well as how the board thinks together.

- Individuals and the group must be even more tolerant, respectful and patient with each other as the board challenges its own assumptions about the impact of its decisions. Diversity is critical—multiple perspectives, expertise across many domains and types of organizations, cultural diversity, demographic diversity, and much more are all critical to shifting the mindset.

- If the Strategic Board looks out toward a distant horizon, the Mindful Board constantly scans 360 degrees of the horizon. Embracing the complexity that comes with mindful deliberations, the board and enterprise are challenged in this transition to measure and evaluate outcomes from several new vantage points.

- Every transition brings a certain "emotional load" for individual board members. As you and your board move along the path, that emotional load increases as commitment and personal accountability increase. In Mindful Board deliberations, the emotional tension arises from staying in and with uncomfortable ambiguity. This is why you have to prepare people for the vulnerability required in conversations. Be prepared for board member turnover.

- You have probably noticed this is a different transition from the first two. Draw from the well of intuition and sensing the dynamics in the room and beyond to guide next steps.

Employ the Six Tools

Flip the Switch to Start the Transition to Mindful Board

Activate Deliberations + Relationships + Membership

This transition can be as dramatic for some boards as the move from Consent to Working Board. Board members will need a foundation of disciplines and capabilities for Mindful governing. As with the first two transitions, this third transition requires actions and strategies to get the process going. Light up the signs and signals generated by board members and senior officers.

Deliberations, relationships and membership are key levers to make this significant leap possible. You have determined the R-Factor is fully present and you and your board are ready to proceed. Here are some suggestions for you to consider.

Expand the Scope of Deliberations

Create "safe space" to consider consequences of decisions. Establish a process for hearing all points of view while managing the time. If people are reluctant to participate, ask them to take the role of key stakeholders and voice their concerns about the organization and its products or services. Draw attention to how deliberations are changing.

Consider starting the transition with a retreat focused on one specific issue and expand the dialogue to consider all the known and potential long-term effects of the decision. Intentionally ask provocative questions that have been ignored or forbidden or "out of scope." Use this time to talk about both sides of the deliberations—the content and the emotions.

Strategic Boards learn to *use experts* to prepare them for deliberations. Mindful Boards use internal and external experts *and* industry outsiders—members of the community or interest groups—to broaden and deepen their discussions. Mindful Boards want to shrink the blind spots and look to multiple sources to enrich deliberations.

From Our Case Files:

 When deciding how aggressively they would pursue a "green strategy," the board and officers debated being on the frontier or a fast follower of other leaders in their "dirty" industry. They brought in environmental scientists to present possible models they could adopt. Other business leaders in the community came to give their impression of the company. The dialogue went on for at least six months. After reviewing several financial models, the board and officers decided they could not afford to be on the leading edge but they could be diligent stewards of their operational processes, quickly learn from others, and generate cleaner air and water.

Strengthen Relationships

"Tolerance, respect, patience" are big words. They are value-rich and weighty. These are words individual board members will most likely interpret and/or live out slightly differently. At the point of launching the transition, *assign an ad hoc group to design and lead a discussion* at a board meeting to address this question: "What is required for a Mindful Board to demonstrate tolerance, respect and patience, particularly in deliberations?" Integrate the distinctions that emerge into board member expectations.

Take extra care *to build in social time* for board members to get to know each other better. Look for opportunities to bring people together in new configurations and offer discussion questions or topics that draw out insights, knowledge and wisdom.

Use scenario planning techniques to allow board members and officers to talk about important uncertainties. Up until now, speaking openly about worries and future unknowns that will impact the organization is unusual. To normalize such discussions use three common scenario tools: Business as Usual, Impending Nightmare, and Fortuitous Breakthrough. Think through a contingency plan for each of the relevant scenarios. Then the group is ready to stand together when a scenario begins to unfold.

Establish mechanisms and norms for "stopping the action" in meetings if the intensity turns from deep inquiry into win-lose debate.

The three scenarios have themes over the next 3-5 years. **Business as Usual** means the organization's performance doesn't get better or worse than current measurements, even if contexts change. **Impending Nightmare** allows the team to talk about the big uncertainties that scare them enough to worry about the organization's survival. **Fortuitous Breakthrough** is an insight, innovation, or acquisition that changes the identity and potential of the organization so it can leapfrog in its performance. Scenario planning requires the team to gather data to prove their hypothesis, identify a monitoring system, and offer a contingency plan for each scenario.

Adjust and Adapt Membership to the Fourth Stage

Start with assessing how much you and your board see, *recognize, and tap the diversity of expertise, wisdom and perspective of the current group of directors or trustees.* Test your knowledge and access against the critical issues facing the enterprise.

Step up and help members who are having difficulty with this transition. Perhaps a mentor or "board buddy" can help that person talk about and think through how to adjust to the new way of deliberating. It can also mean helping someone see if they are no longer a good fit for the emerging board.

Stretch member expectations. Give your board a head start by recruiting members who know how to contribute to Mindful conversations. Find ways to keep practical, operational members engaged and involved. When evaluating board performance and individual director contributions include questions about participation in Mindful dialogue.

Power Up to Transform into the Mindful Board

Use All the Tools:
Purpose+Tasks+Structures+Relationships+Membership+Deliberations

This is the point in the transformation to Mindful Board when a serious upgrading of all of the six elements is critical. Think of it as an interior renovation that requires everyone's participation. The relationship between the board and the CEO and senior officers can become rocky, so stay attuned to signals. Creativity, self-awareness and exquisite communication are required to avoid turning this point in the transformation into confusion and frustration.

Again, here are some ideas to get you started.

Distinguish the Unique Purpose of a Mindful Board

Create a working group to define your board's rationale and practice of Mindful governance. Include the officer group in crafting a statement of purpose that clearly describes what is important and why your board needs to be a Mindful Board. Include a description of how the critical work of Consent, Working and Strategic responsibilities will get done at this fourth stage. Bring this back to the full board and take the time—perhaps over several meetings—to refine and adopt their statement.

Document the board's mindful decisions in ways that go beyond meeting minutes. Focus on the process: What happened and how did you get to the final decision? Recall the idea of an annual report on board performance suggested for the first two transitions. That report can become a vital record of how mindful governance has shaped decisions and outcomes.

Redesign Tasks and Structures Creatively and Intentionally

Key tasks in all four stages of governance will be completed and the capabilities carried forward by the board and officers. New tasks include looking through all the "windows" to understand the contexts in which the organization exists, making sense of the weak signals coming from a distance, envisioning the organization in perpetuity, choosing a strategic direction with the help of the officers, and mastering adaptive leadership.

New tasks require new structures. The board meeting agenda becomes a vital structure to support all the work that needs to be done. The chair must identify a group who will balance responsiveness and continuity in designing each agenda. The executive committee may be the responsible group; however, a group separate from the formal power structure can be very helpful by representing each governance stage.

Most committees are ad hoc, while core fiduciary committees still stand (audit, governance, and compensation and evaluation). Each board must prioritize its work for the next several months and figure out how the work will get done in the available time.

Make sure the CEO and senior officers articulate the impact the transformation is having on their roles and relationship with the board, and how the partnership is evolving. This may require a focused conversation to assure the board and officers stay aligned and not detached from each other.

Develop and Apply the Disciplines

Utilize Reflection to Recognize When Things Go Wrong

Reflection is critical during this third transition. Mindful conversations and decision-making have the potential to go wrong when board members—especially board leaders and the CEO—get nervous. The conversation may feel out of control or irrelevant. Or, someone emphasizes that inevitable "Now what do we do?!" In the transition and transformation to Mindful Board, everyone, and especially the board chair, must create and sustain the "safe space." The safe space makes it easier to manage the tensions and worries that arise when the path forward is not perfectly clear.

Statements from members and officers that signal "something has gone wrong" in this transition:

- "This feels too theoretical. Can we get back to work?"

- "I don't know how I can contribute to this conversation."

- "We're losing sight of the day-to-day business and strategy."

- "We need to be practical. The future will take care of itself."

- "The situation is too complex for us to take up. Leave it to the executives."

As leadership by the group is maturing, the chair's role as integrator and facilitator becomes increasingly important. Everyone is a mindful board member at this stage; the board chair is the orchestra conductor who leads and helps the music sing. Encourage the discipline of reflection by everyone when the process falters.

See Success—Big and Small

Again, apply our idea: write an annual statement of board performance and progress towards becoming a Mindful Board. Include officers on the work group assigned to write the annual statement. This document is for the board and officers and should be treated as confidential. It brings successes and what the board has learned to the foreground. Consider evaluating the board and officers' performance as the governance community. Again, another use of Reflection.

As your success builds, commission a business school to write a case study for internal management training, or publish an article about the journey and significance of the board's transformation.

Manage the Momentum

In Chapter 2 we describe the risks if a board gets stuck in Mindful Board when the context changes. Managing momentum at this stage centers on the connection among fiduciary responsibilities, operational reality, vital strategy, and the long term consequences. Clear priorities and tasks give context for each board member's contribution as the board expands its capacity to function in higher degrees of complexity. Maintaining a culture of reflection and trustworthy relationships reinforces momentum.

Personal Commitment

Board transformation cannot occur without the personal commitment of every board member, the CEO and all the senior officers. There comes a point in the process when purposefully asking for individual, personal commitment to the transformation process is critical. This request is as powerful as asking for a vote on major issue or asking for a significant donation. Don't bypass this act of engagement or assume everyone is still onboard with the transformation. Ask.

Continue to develop the board's membership as a diverse group of people who care deeply about the organization's mission and its success. As people come on and leave the board, the governance committee must be diligent about building and maintaining a community of directors or trustees who are capable of all four stages of governance.

❧

Prescient Ponders the Mindful Board

It's certainly hard to believe the Consent Board we first met could even consider making the last transition and transformation into the Mindful Board. There is nothing more powerful than the press of the external contexts, the looming possibility of new leadership, and the willingness to look at the impact of decisions to prompt new possibilities.

Know the impact of your decisions

George finds himself adjusting to the role of board chair with humility and a healthy dose of anxiety. One more board member, Bob, has decided it's time to "retire" from the board. The newest open seat once again provokes a sense of loss and also presents an opportunity. Based on a recommendation by Dave, the Chief Operating Officer, George has decided to schedule a board retreat to evaluate the strategic moves Prescient has made recently and what the future holds George pulls a retreat design team together.

On his way to the design team meeting George reflects on how his participation from a new "seat" is profoundly different and a bit unsettling. He laughs out loud when he realizes that instead of him recommending the retreat, the request had come from a key officer.

The group suggests an outside speaker to kick off the retreat. They suggest a futurist to speak to "hard trends and soft trends" from a global megatrends level as a way to open up the dialogue early on.

With all that rumbling around in his head, George walks into the board meeting. This is his third board meeting as chair. In the space of three hours, three board members raise unsettling questions. Sophia stops the action in the middle of a discussion of finances to assert, "We need to review our vendor list and our investment portfolio. Are we comfortable who we are doing business with?" That certainly prompts a lively discussion!

Then, not too long afterwards, Charles speaks up during a review of recent initiatives. Charles, a local leader and regional statesman, comments, "You need to know there appear to be negative consequences to our latest actions associated with these initiatives. Community leaders are very concerned. I got a call from the governor. And last night our Senator called me to say we're being discussed in Washington."

And lastly, Eliza and Sean together raise the possibility that Prescient could play a true global leadership role if only Prescient would look hard at exactly how the business model is impacting communities and beyond. They throw out a view ideas A tad fuzzy, their nascent ideas grab everyone's attention.

The complex issue of impact on communities, regions and societies is alive and well within the Prescient board that morning.

Take a break and hold your breath

During the break, Jim pulls George aside. "Don't forget to tell them." George sighs. "Right. Thanks for the reminder."

The board reconvenes. George starts the second half of the meeting by informing the board that Prescient is poised to continue thriving. He also announces that Jim has decided that it is time for him to retire. Sidebar conversations erupt and a general discussion follows. George steps in to move the discussion forward, "We have just been talking about the impact of our decisions on the world outside of the boundaries of Prescient. Now we need to face the impact of our next big decision. We must think together and work together as we consider the impact of the next CEO to our many constituents and—dare I say it—the world."

Little did they know then just how much those wise words influenced the future until many years later.

What we see happening

Look beyond the leadership changes and the entrance of the new board member to see what has been happening to Prescient. To be sure these changes shook up the situation—a phenomenon that can be very helpful. From the balcony perspective, Prescient's board and officer group have mastered attunement to the external context and multiple influences. As a board, the group has developed the six disciplines over time and so far uses them well. The disciplines will be very helpful as the board and new CEO wrestle with how Prescient moves forward in a highly complex environment.

George as board chair makes sense at this point in time. He is comfortable with facilitating deep dialogue and engaging board members. Prescient's board and officers will now need to stretch themselves even further. They must figure out what being a Mindful Board means to them within their industry at this time. It looks like they have all talents and resources needed to make the last transition. The new COO, Dave, and the prospect of a new CEO are both exciting and scary developments. During this time of operational changes George and all board members must keep the conversation going about board's emerging *purpose* as critical to a sustainable future.

இ

Continue to Build *Your* Model of Conscious Governance

One of the biggest challenges for lots of people on boards is changing how they think of themselves. They don't expect to have to face challenges. They just want to meet basic shareholder expectations and move on. Sometimes they expect officers or other board members, especially the chair, to ensure all matters are well handled. This is antiquated. Legal standards and public expectations of accountability have risen substantially over the past decade.

— CEO and Board Chair and Client

Make the Landscape of Conscious Governance Yours

From the first brush stroke in Chapter 1 all the way through Chapter 9 we have painted the landscape of Conscious Governance for you. To help you understand the Mindful Board, we have brought you along the path—from opening the door to giving you a balcony perspective where the far horizon is alight with extraordinary purpose and discernment. It is a landscape of transition and transformation.

What you now do with what you have read is up to you. The opportunity is at hand.

Lean into the Journey with an Open Heart

In their 2002 book, *Leadership on the Line,* Ronald Heifetz and Marty Linsky challenge us to accept the power of an open heart when exercising our leadership.

"A sacred heart is an antidote to one of the most common and destructive 'solutions' to the challenges of modern life: numbing oneself. Leading with an open heart helps you stay alive in your soul. It enables you to feel faithful to whatever is true, including doubt, without fleeing, acting out, or reaching for a quick fix. Moreover, the power of a sacred heart helps you to mobilize others to do the same—to face challenges that demand courage, and to endure the pains of change without deceiving themselves or running away." (p. 230)

Whether you are a board member, board chair, CEO, officer or bystander, becoming the Mindful Board calls us to stay open, persistent and *mindful.*

Be a Mindful Person

As you reflect on what you have read, notice what you learned and what may have triggered a memory from your own experiences. Notice what you disagree with and articulate your reasons. Identify the most important characteristics of the Mindful Board in your model. Clarify your model for leading a significant change along the four phases along the *Continuum of Conscious Governance.*

Your own journey will take shape—your customized landscape will come into focus and you will know the way forward. Look for the signposts we have given you, make choices that work for you, and take time to celebrate the milestones. Make the landscape of Conscious Governance yours. Above all, keep learning. Practice being a mindful person whenever (and wherever) you are serving those around you. Apply the concepts, tools and action ideas in this book to the many facets of your life. The principles and practices are not confined to the boardroom.

We, too, are still learning and discovering how the Mindful Board is a model for governing *and* living. It's worth the effort—for now and the future.

We will continue to share what we are learning, stories from fellow travelers, and practical suggestions. You will find these on our website *themindfulboard.com.* See you there.

Appendix

Books and Articles Mentioned in this Book

Chapter 1

Murray, Alan. 2007. *Revolt in the Boardroom: The new rules of power in corporate America*. New York: HarperCollins Publishers.

Raelin, Joseph A. 2003. *Creating Leaderful Organizations: How to Bring Out Leadership in Everyone*. San Francisco: Berrett-Koehler.

Smith, David H. 1995. *Entrusted: The Moral Responsibilities of Trusteeship*. Bloomington, IN: Indiana University Press.

Casal, Christian, and Christian Caspar. February, 2014. "Building a forward-looking board." McKinsey & Company Quarterly (on line).

Charan, Ram, Dennis Carey, and Michael Useem. 2014. *Boards that Lead: When to Take Charge, When to Partner, and When to Stay Out of the Way*. Boston: Harvard Business School Publishing Corporation.

Chapter 2

Charan, Ram. 2005. *Boards that Deliver*. San Francisco: Jossey-Bass.

Chait, Richard P., William P. Ryan, and Barbara E. Taylor. 2005. *Governance as Leadership: Reframing the Work of Nonprofit Boards*. Hoboken, NJ: John Wiley & Sons.

Lorsch, Jay W. 2012. *The Future of Boards: Meeting the Governance Challenges of the Twenty-First Century*. Boston: Harvard Business Review Press.

Keith, Kent M. 2011. *Servant Leadership in the Boardroom: Fulfilling the Public Trust*. Westfield, IN: Greenleaf Center for Servant Leadership.

Chapter 3

Senge, Peter M. 1990. *The Fifth Discipline: The Art & Practice of The Learning Organization*. New York: Doubleday.

Chapter 5

Hanh, Thich N. 1975. *The Miracle of Mindfulness: An Introduction to the Practice of Meditation.* Boston: Beacon Press.

Chapter 6

Wheatley, Margaret. 1996. *A Simpler Way.* San Francisco: Berrett-Koehler.

Continue to Build Your Model of Conscious Governance

Heifetz, Ronald A., and Marty Linsky, M. 2002. *Leadership on the Line: Staying Alive through the Dangers of Leading.* Boston: Harvard Business School Press.

Additional Resources

Transforming from one stage to the next on the continuum of Conscious Governance requires tapping into a range of content areas, approaches to managing organizational change efforts, and individual skills. There are many wonderful resources for you to access.

Here are some suggestions from our bookshelves that we have found useful over the years. Each of these categories would yield hundreds of direct and related materials from an internet search. We found a few resources we think are useful on the journey.

Governance

Beyond Certainty by Charles Handy (Harvard Business School Press, 1995)

Creating Caring & Capable Board: Reclaiming the Passion for Active Trusteeship by Katherine Tyler Scott (Jossey-Bass, 2000)

Effective Governing Boards: A Guide for Members of Governing Boards of Independent Colleges and Universities (Association of Governing Boards Press, 2009)

Healing the Heart of Democracy by Parker J. Palmer (Jossey-Bass, 2011)

Leadership and Governance from the Inside Out edited by Robert Gandossy and Jeffrey Sonnenfeld (Wiley & Sons, 2004)

The Mindful Board by Charlotte Roberts and Martha Summerville (strategy+business, January, 25, 2016) *http://www.strategy-business.com/article/The-Mindful-Board?gko=97a18*

Trustees as Servants by Robert Greenleaf (Windy Row Press, 1974)

Organization Change

Designing Organizations: Strategy, Structure and Process at the Business Unit and Enterprise Levels by Jay R. Galbraith (Jossey-Bass, 2014)

Great by Choice by Jim Collins and Morten Hansen (HarperCollins Publishers, 2011)

Immunity to Change by Robert Kegan and Lisa Laskow Lahey (Harvard Business School Publishing Corporation, 2009)

Thinking in Systems by Danella Meadows, edited by Diana Wright (Sustainability Institute, 2008)

"We Still Don't Know the Difference between Change and Transformation" by Ron Asheknas (Harvard Business Review, on line, January 25, 2015)

Group Decision Making

Calling the Circle by Christina Baldwin (Swan Raven & Company, 1994)

Crucial Conversations: Tool for Talking When Stakes Are High by Kerry Patterson, Joseph Grenny, Ron McMillan, and Al Switzler (McGraw-Hill Books, 2012)

Culture of Inquiry: Healthy Debate in the Boardroom by Nancy Axelrod (Board-Source, 2007)

Divide or Conquer: How Great Teams Turn Conflict into Strength by Diana McLain Smith (Penguin Group, 2008)

Humble Inquiry: The Gentle Art of Asking Instead of Telling by Edgar Schein (Berrett-Koehler Publishers, 2013)

Practicing Discernment Together by Lon Fendall, Jan Wood and Bruce Bishop (Barclay Press, 2007)

The Wisdom of Group Decisions: 100 Principles and Practical Tips for Collaboration by Craig Freshley (Good Group Decisions, 2010)

You Don't Have to Do It Alone by Richard Axelrod, Emily Axelrod, Julie Beedon, and Robert Jacobs (Berrett-Koehler Publishers, 2004)

Being a Mindful Board Member

A Balcony Perspective: Clarifying the Trustee Role by Richard Broholm and Douglas Wysockey-Johnson (Centered Life, 2004)

Called to Serve by Max De Pree (Wm. B. Eerdmans Publishing Co., 2001)

The Heart Aroused: Poetry and the Preservation of the Soul in Corporate America by David Whyte (Currency Doubleday, 2002)

The Servant Leader Within: A Transformative Path by Robert Greenleaf, edited by Beazley, Beggs and Spears (Paulist Press, 2003)

The Unique Double Servant Leadership Role of the Board Chairperson by John Carver (The Greenleaf Center, 1999)

The Mindful Board Website

Visit our website—themindfulboard.com—for additional tools, ideas and comments from executives who have lead board transformation efforts.

Work Team Trust Survey

In describing the discipline of trustworthiness in Chapter 5 (Become the Mindful Board Member) we mention the 21 characteristics of trustworthiness. Here is the survey tool you can use with your board as you develop this discipline.

An important element of an learning executive team is trust. Learning can be a high stakes situation. Trust is defined as "confident reliance on another." How well do you trust your current executive team members?

The following behavioral descriptions were identified from interviews of over 300 managers.

Complete the following questions with each team member in mind. Indicate how strongly you agree or disagree on a scale of 1-6.

> 1 = very strongly disagree   4 = mildly agree
> 2 = moderately disagree   5 = moderately agree
> 3 = mildly disagree   6 - very strongly agree

____ I have a good idea how my team member will act; he/she is consistent.

____ I believe my team member is dependable; he/she keeps agreements, commitments, and promises.

____ I feel my team member would not intentionally hurt me in any way; he/she demonstrates caring for others.

____ I have faith that my team member will act in my best interest even if I am not present; we share common values and goals.

____ I know my team member can do the work we have identified; he/she does high quality work.

____ I think my team member's words are true; he/she is honest.

____ I hear my team member's words as authentic; he/she says what he/she means.

____ I know my team member will admit mistakes and fears; he/she is open.

____ I can share my crazy ideas and deep feelings with my team member; he/she is non-judgmental.

____ I am not afraid of uncertainty in our future; my team member and I can figure out most anything.

____ I am comfortable with the investment (social, emotional, psychological) I have made in this relationship; my team member respects the relationship.

____ I don't mind asking my team member for help in understanding a new process, a policy, etc.; he/she is a good coach.

____ I openly receive feedback from my team member; his/her feedback is direct, specific, and non-punishing.

____ I am willing to suspend my position to understand my team member's point of view; he/she can make a valuable contribution.

____ I know my team member suspends his/her position to understand me; he/she believes I can make a valuable contribution.

____ I can freely disagree with my team member; he/she is equally committed to uncovering the truth and the best solution.

____ I listen to criticism from my team member; he/she does not have a need to "win" or be better.

____ I feel confirmed by my team member; he/she accepts me as I am and does not demand I play a particular role.

____ I enjoy a free-flowing dialogue with my team member; we blend our thoughts well together for a better understanding.

____ I have fun with my team member; he/she shares a common spirit.

____ My team member has told me that I can trust him/her.

____ Other (Please describe your criteria.)

72178247R00102

Made in the USA
Middletown, DE
03 May 2018